Helping the Severely Handicapped Child

HELPING
THE SEVERELY
HANDICAPPED
CHILD

A Guide for Parents and Teachers

Phyllis B. Doyle
John F. Goodman
Jeffery N. Grotsky
Lester Mann

Illustrations by Joseph E. Connolly

JOHN DAY BOOKS IN
S E
SPECIAL EDUCATION

THOMAS Y. CROWELL, PUBLISHERS

Established 1834

New York

This guide is a completely revised and expanded edition of an earlier work, prepared for distribution in Pennsylvania only. The former version, entitled *How to Help Your Child: A Guide for Parents of Multiply Handicapped Children,* was funded under a grant from the United States Office of Education, Bureau of Education for the Handicapped (grant number G007503427).

FIRST EDITION

Designed by Stephanie Winkler

Library of Congress Cataloging in Publication Data

Main entry under title:
    Helping the severely handicapped child.
        "Revised and expanded edition of . . . How to help your child."
        "A John Day book."
        Bibliography: p.
        1. Handicapped children—Case and treatment— Handbooks, manuals, etc. 2. Handicapped children—
Rehabilitation—Handbooks, manuals, etc. I. Doyle, Phyllis B.
HV 888.H68 1979   362.7'8'4   78-3300
ISBN 0-381-90063-0

79 80 81 82 83 10 9 8 7 6 5 4 3 2 1

Contents

Introduction

This guide has been written to help you help your severely handicapped child—a child with severe physical impairments who is also mentally retarded. To be most useful to you, the guide uses simple, straightforward language.

The information the guide contains is based on three questions often asked by parents of severely handicapped children: What is the public school doing to help my child? What can I do at home to help my child? And where can I find the special help he or she needs?* These three questions are answered in the first three parts of the guide. Part IV explains some legal aspects of your child's education.

Part I describes a public school training program for severely handicapped children. All handicapped children of school age in this country now have the right to a free public education. Part IV shows how this has come about and what it means for you as a parent. Because the schools must now provide suitable training programs for handicapped children, we have described one of these programs to show you how it could help your child.

Part II of the guide explains how you can help your child at home and teach him to do things for himself. For example, there are hints on how to feed your child, how to toilet train him, and how to teach him to dress himself.

Part III outlines the information you may need in order to find help for your child. It includes information on how to find a qualified babysitter, what tax deductions you can claim, and how to make special equipment. We have provided a full listing of special services and agencies.

This guide is only a beginning. It does not contain all the information you need to educate and care for your child. However, it can be a base of information on which you can build. To help you learn more, we have included

---

* This is the last time we will use the phrase *he or she*. From now on, for simplicity's sake, we will alternate *he* and *she*, chapter by chapter.

reading lists throughout the book on subjects discussed and a bibliography of other reading material on the severely handicapped at the end.

So, after you read the guide, be sure to talk to your child's doctor and his teacher and therapists at school. Talk to the people at the local agencies for the handicapped. And talk to other parents of severely handicapped children.

You should keep in contact with these people and work with them. Through their assistance and the information in this guide, you can give your child the help he needs.

PART I

Helping Your Child Get the Most out of School

The most important way to help your child in his school program is to understand something about the training that goes on in his classroom every day.

Part I examines a public school training program for severely handicapped children. Here you will see what the children do during the day—from the time they get off the bus in the morning until they head home again in the afternoon. To get a really clear idea of what *your* child does at school, talk to his teacher and, of course, visit the school. She can tell you about his training program and how you can help. Your child's training will be most successful when you and his teacher work together. Cooperation is the key.

"Benjamin! Good morning!"

Benjamin grins and looks out the window of his minibus. A teacher slides open the side door and reaches in to help him unbuckle his seatbelt and shoulder strap. She takes him by the hand and helps him step down from the bus.

Another teacher climbs into the bus and unbuckles the straps around Eileen, who sits in a padded plastic carseat. Eileen rides in the carseat because she is severely handicapped and can't sit up in a regular bus seat. The teacher cradles Eileen in her arms and carries her into the building.

There will be very few children in your child's class—no more than six or seven. This allows the teacher and her assistant to give a lot of individual attention to each pupil. Your child's class is also arranged so that the children in it can learn from each other. For example, it is helpful for a child who is

beginning to walk to be with other children who can already walk. He will watch and learn from them.

Many people contribute to a successful classroom experience for your child. The trained teacher has knowledge of your child's abilities and needs, and she calls upon speech, language, vision, physical, and occupational therapists to help your child overcome his problems and learn new skills.

As the teacher carries Eileen into the classroom, she checks her diapers and notices that the child is wet. So she lays Eileen on a padded tabletop and begins to change her diapers.

Placed around the classroom is furniture specially suited to the needs of the children. A little boy who has difficulty holding his head up sits in a wheelchair with a headrest. Another boy sits on a potty-chair with a seatbelt to keep him from falling off and armrests to help him sit up.

Helping the teacher with the children is the teacher's assistant. "Here we

go, Michelle," the assistant says as she picks up the girl and lays her on her stomach on a "wedge"—a large wedge-shaped piece of foam rubber covered with cloth. When Michelle is placed in this position, she can learn to control her body. Then she can lift her head and look at her surroundings.

During the day your child works on activities to help him learn how to take care of himself. Included are such things as holding a spoon, picking up his head, using the toilet, and pushing his arm through a sleeve.

Since your child's class is small, the teacher is able to plan a training program just for him. To do this, she uses reports from doctors and the school psychologists. These reports often give information about your child which can be used to understand him better. More important, your child's teacher tries to understand what he does and why he does it by carefully watching his behavior. These are the first steps in developing a training program for your child.

The teacher pushes the hair back from Amy's face. Amy is a new student, and the teacher wants to find out if she can undress and dress herself. By observing Amy's dressing behavior, the teacher will have a better idea of how to teach the child to dress herself.

5

Since Amy has just arrived, it is a good time for the teacher to find out if she can take her coat off. "Take your coat off, Amy." Amy looks up at the teacher but doesn't move. Now the teacher pulls the coat sleeve off one arm. "Amy, take your coat off." She doesn't move. So now the teacher takes the coat off, stopping at certain points to tell her what to do and then watching to see if she responds.

"Take your arm out. . . . Take arm out, Amy." Amy doesn't respond to the directions. However, the teacher sees that when her arm is almost out of the sleeve that she tries to pull it out without help. So, Amy is given a hug for trying. This is a reward that helps her learn.

The teacher writes down what Amy has done. This information will help her develop future plans for teaching Amy how to undress and dress herself.

The information that the teacher records about what your child can or cannot do before training is marked on a chart or graph. The chart helps the teacher decide where training should begin. From this starting point, the line on the chart will rise and fall, depending on how your child does each day. This type of day-to-day recordkeeping is important because it tells the teacher how well the training program is going. If it isn't going too well, she may teach your child something simpler or try the same thing with him in a different way. The chart also helps the teacher show you what your child has learned and what he still needs to learn.

To help your child learn, the teacher rewards him with praise, affectionate hugs, good things to eat, and toys. Anything a child is willing to work for may be used as a reward. Rewards, properly used, help improve behavior. Rewarding a child for good behavior is an excellent and pleasant way to help him learn.

Two little girls sit at a small table with the teacher between them. They have just finished lunch, and a spoon and a cup remain on the table. Today the teacher wants to find out if they know the meaning of the words "cup" and "spoon." The teacher places the cup and the spoon in front of Eileen.

"Eileen, spoon. Touch spoon." At first Eileen looks away from the table. Then she looks back at the spoon and slowly reaches out and touches it. "Good girl, Eileen!" The teacher rewards her with praise. The teacher asks her to touch the spoon a few more times and rewards her for trying. Eileen's progress is then recorded on her chart.

Next, the teacher places a cup and spoon on the table in front of Jamie. "Jamie, touch spoon." Jamie reaches out and touches the spoon. "Good girl. Good, Jamie!" Up until today, the teacher had been giving Jamie a little bite of cereal as a reward for touching the spoon. But today she wants to

see if Jamie will do it without the food reward. So she just gives the child a word of praise as a reward. The teacher says, "Jamie, touch cup." Jamie looks up at the teacher, then at the table. She slowly reaches out and touches the cup. "Good, Jamie! Good girl!"

The training program that the teacher sets up for your child is based on objectives. An objective is a specific goal that the teacher sets for your child. For example, an objective for your child might be "to pick up a cup of juice, bring it to his mouth without spilling it, and drink the juice."

To make it easier for your child to reach the objective, the teacher breaks it down into smaller steps. She teaches your child one step at a time. For example, she might teach him to just pick up the cup. As he learns each step, she helps him put it together with what he has already learned. Finally he is able to do the whole thing; he has reached the objective.

During an average day, your child's teacher might work with him on several different objectives. One objective might be in the area of feeding, another in toilet training, another in communication, and so on. As the teacher works on each of the objectives, she keeps a careful record of your child's progress. The teacher—and you—can look at this record and see how well your child is doing.

"OK, Marie. Let's have something to drink." The teacher places Marie's hands around a plastic two-handled cup. "Marie, drink." Marie lifts the cup to her mouth and takes a drink of apricot juice—one of her favorites. "Good! Good drinking, Marie."

The teacher has been working with Leonard and Marie on the objective of drinking from a cup for about three months now. Leonard is not as far along as Marie, but the teacher works with each child as an individual, and his improvement is only compared to his past work, not to other children's.

Sitting behind Leonard, the teacher takes his hands in hers and helps him hold the cup. "Leonard, drink." Holding his hands on the cup, the teacher lifts it to his mouth and tips it slightly. Then she watches to see if the juice is going into Leonard's mouth. As Leonard begins to sip, she takes away her hands so that he is holding the cup by himself. Yesterday, when the teacher tried this, Leonard dropped the cup and juice went all over his bib. But today, he holds the cup to his lips and goes on sipping the juice. "Good job, Leonard!"

Although your child spends most of his school day with the teacher and her assistant, speech, vision, physical and occupational therapists may also work with him.

The *speech therapist* tries to help your child learn how to talk. First, she trains him to use his lips and tongue to make sounds. Then she helps him

put the sounds together into words. Like the other therapists, the speech therapist works with the teacher to develop a special program for your child.

If your child is blind, the *vision therapist* can help him learn to use his other senses. She may, for example, teach him to know food by smell or touch, and to identify objects by the sounds they make. If a child is not blind but has poor vision, the therapist can help him learn to focus on objects or to follow moving objects with his eyes. This kind of training helps him learn to do other things like feeding or dressing himself.

9

The *physical therapist* can help your child learn how to control his body. She can show your child's teacher exercises to strengthen his muscles and help him use them more effectively. She helps the child learn to sit up, crawl, walk, and use stairs. She also checks braces and wheelchairs to make sure they are just right for him. When your child begins to outgrow his braces or wheelchair, the therapist can also give you advice about changes that need to be made or new equipment you might need to buy.

The *occupational therapist* can help your child learn how to take better care of himself. She might work with him on things like brushing his hair or feeding himself. She helps him learn to control the movement of his body. And she might use games to help your child learn to follow directions more accurately, to finish what he starts, and to use his eyes and hands more effectively.

The school also has a *social worker,* who will help you understand more fully what goes on in the school. She will meet with you alone or with a group of other parents, and will tell you about the school program and what other kinds of help you can get for your child.

Probably the best way for you to understand what your child is doing in school is by meeting with his teacher. Regular meetings with the teacher will help you become more involved and more familiar with your child's progress and problems at school. Your child's teacher can also give you some ideas about how to help him at home.

When you come in for a parent-teacher meeting, it might be helpful to bring along any questions you have about your child's behavior, or any ideas you have about his training. By preparing for your conference in this way, you will be better able to work with the teacher.

The door to the classroom swings open and Mr. and Mrs. Eckert walk in. Miss Berger, the teacher, sees them, smiles, and points toward a couple of chairs. At the moment she is busy with their son, Benjamin. "Benjamin, touch head." She places her hands on his and guides them to his head.

The parents watch as Miss Berger moves around the circle of children seated in the middle of the room. This is "circle hour," the last activity of the day. Today, during circle hour, the children are being taught the parts of the body. Each one practices touching his head, ears, or nose. Finally, circle hour ends with a song: "If you're happy and you know it, clap your hands. . . ."

The teacher and her assistant help the children into their coats and onto the bus. Then the assistant sits down to play with Benjamin while the teacher meets with his parents. She lays out on the table several charts that show Benjamin's progress over the last three months.

Miss Berger points to one of the charts. "You see, he can pick up finger foods and put them in his mouth, which is really an improvement since the beginning of the year.''

Mr. Eckert, who has brought a list of questions and comments, agrees. "We've noticed the same thing at home. And it's made dinner time a little easier for us." Mrs. Eckert breaks in, "Do you think he's ready to spoon-feed himself?''

"I think we may be ready to start working with him on it," Miss Berger says. "But it can be slow going. Maybe we'll just start getting him used to holding the spoon.''

"How about dressing himself?" Mr. Eckert asks.

Miss Berger shakes her head and smiles. "Well, we haven't had much luck there, have we?''

"No," says Mrs. Eckert. "But I wanted to tell you something. Last week, as I was taking his coat off, he helped me by pulling his arm out." She looks at her notebook. "It was twice last week, in fact. Wednesday and Friday.''

Miss Berger raises her eyebrows. "Really? I'm glad you told me because I

hadn't noticed anything like that at school. I'll see if I can get him to pull his arm out when I take his coat off at school."

The discussion moves from dressing to toilet training and then to Benjamin's most recent check-up at the dentist. Finally, all the items on Mr. Eckert's list are checked off. He looks up at Miss Berger and says, "Well, I think that's all for now—do you have anything more for us?"

"Yes, I want to thank you both for working with me on the training. It really helps me . . . and Benjamin."

PART II

How to Help Your
Child at Home

You spend a large part of your day moving, feeding, and dressing your child. There are ways of making these activities easier for you and for her. At the same time, these activities can become real learning experiences for your child.

In Part II, we offer suggestions for these activities. We have also included some comments on play and recreation, sexual concerns, and the rest of the family. Our suggestions are general and may not be exactly right for your child. But, with help from your child's teacher, therapists, and doctor, you can tailor these activities to your child's needs.

Communication

Communication is always a "two-way street." Or, as we say, it consists of input and output. Input is hearing, seeing, touching—that is, the flow of information from the senses to the brain. Output is talking, writing, or gesturing—using information that comes from the brain. Between the input and output stages the brain must use language and thought. This means that the child must "classify" information which the brain receives and respond to it.

For example, what happens when you hear the doorbell? You hear the sound of the bell and classify it as the doorbell. You think about what it means (someone is at the door), then you respond (by asking a family member to answer the door or by going yourself). These actions involve language and thought.

And to have language and thought your child needs to have experience. She needs experience in using her senses, like hearing, touching, and seeing, so that she can recognize sounds and sights. She needs experience in hearing words to describe objects and events, so that she can learn these words. She needs experience in hearing how words are put together so she'll know how to understand and think with these words. She needs experience in knowing how to choose words that will say what she means to say. And she needs experience in talking and saying things to people. It is important for you to understand that a child can have language and can continue to develop language without being able to speak. Language is considered to be the understanding of words; and speech is the actual production of sounds to form words. (For a full discussion of language, see the book written by Kathryn Horton listed at the end of this chapter.)

Try to provide exposure for your child to situations which a normal child would experience. Young children learn a lot from exploring their environment and experimenting with objects in it. They may pick up, throw, chew, drop, and pound objects. If your child is unable to do some of these things

15

because of her physical handicap, you can help her by showing her objects and helping her to manipulate them as a normal child would.

Talk about what is happening at the moment. If she is crawling across the floor and bumps into something, she may either stop to look at it or go around it. You might say, "See the truck" or "You are crawling around the truck." You could also ask her to pause and look at the truck. This will help your child learn to attach meaning to her experiences. The more you communicate with your child—that is, the more you talk and gesture to her—the more likely she is to learn how to communicate with you.

When you talk to your child, you help her learn to attach meaning to her experiences and you help her learn how to say words and use them in a meaningful way.

Even though she may not seem to respond, tell her what you are doing as you do things around the house—from cooking dinner to watching a football game on television. You should also talk to her while you are doing things together. Use words, gestures, actions, and facial expressions to help her begin to understand what is going on around her.

Your child's teacher and therapists can give you suggestions on how you can help your child learn to communicate. We have also provided some suggestions that will help.

GESTURES

Using gestures gives your child extra input that will help her learn the meaning of words and actions. It's a way to let your child know what you are doing, and what you would like her to do. It also gives her a way to communicate with you if she isn't using words. Consistent, meaningful gestures will lead to understanding if repeated often enough.

To teach your child to use gestures, begin with one you know she can learn quickly. For example, to teach her to let you know she wants to be picked up, raise your arms and say the word "up." If your child imitates you by raising her arms, pick her up and reward her. Show her that you understand and appreciate what she has done.

If she doesn't raise her arms on her own, help her raise them and then say "up" and pick her up. By making certain that you use the same gesture every time, you will keep your child from becoming confused. If she starts to raise her arms when it is time to go to dinner or go outside, pick her up quickly and reward her. She is showing that she understands the connection between the gesture of raising her arms and getting picked up.

SPEECH

While you are helping your child use gestures to communicate, you can also teach her to use sounds or words.

Talk to your child during the day on a regular and informal basis. This will help her to become better acquainted with everyday conversation. Also, remember that it is not only what you say to your child that is important, but how you say it as well. You can use the tone of your voice to communicate how you feel to your child. If you're sorry or if you are pleased, your words, the tone of your voice, and the expression on your face will let her know how you feel.

You can use your conversations with your child to teach her words. For example, when you give her something to eat, you can make it a learning activity by saying the word "eat" slowly, clearly and directly to her as you help her eat. Whenever possible, try to get her to say words after you say them. If she tries to say the word but says it incorrectly, don't scold her or

say "no." Just repeat the word and reward her for trying to say it.

During the day, you will probably have many chances to use words that tell your child what you are doing or what is happening. For example, say "coat" as you take her coat from the closet. Repeat "bath" as you place your child in the tub, or "car" as you put her in the car. By using words to describe actions or objects at hand and by repeating them slowly and clearly, you help your child begin to connect them with the ideas, actions, or objects they represent.

You can often help her understand more clearly what is going on by adding gestures to give extra meaning to the words you use. For instance, if you say the word "tall" you can show what you mean by stretching your arm in the air. However, you should use the same gesture for the same word all the time. This way you not only make your child familiar with both the word and the gesture, but you also avoid confusing her. It may also help if, when you talk to your child, you move her body to help her understand what the word means. Hold her hand out in the rain when you say the word "rain." Or guide her hand to pet a dog as you say "dog."

It will take some children a long time to develop speech, and others will not develop speech at all. In either case it is important for the child to have a way to communicate so that she can express her needs and continue to develop language. A child can have an understanding and ability to use language even though she may not be able to talk (use speech). There are systems of gestures which have been developed to help children without speech learn to communicate. If you are interested in teaching your child gestures, talk to her speech therapist or teacher for more information on how to proceed.

COMMUNICATION BOARDS

Communication boards can be made in any size and shape, depending upon the child's needs. They usually look like small square trays with pictures or words glued to the surface. The child can use the board to communicate by pointing to a picture. For example, one of the pictures could be of food, and the child could point to it when she feels hungry. Or there could be a picture of a sad face, and the child could point to it to indicate when she is feeling unhappy.

Each communication board must be individually developed, its content based upon the child's physical and intellectual abilities. The design of the board will depend upon what sitting position, what method of response (pointing, using eyes), and what placement of the material will permit the most accurate and rapid response.

The content of the boards must be specialized to meet the child's needs in different communication situations. There might be several different boards for different situations. One board may have words used more in the home, one may be for school.

The materials you would need to make a communication board are inexpensive and easy to work with—a tray, some heavy paper, and some plexiglas or other clear washable covering. You can buy electronic communication boards, but they are expensive so carefully evaluate the advantages of this type of board before buying one.

USING SIGNS

While a child is learning to talk, it is also possible to teach her to use signs. Signs consist of conventionally understood gestures, for instance, movements made with the hands. Again, the idea is to give the child a way to communicate and to develop language while she is learning to use speech meaningfully. However, some children may not learn to talk at all, and they will have to depend on signs to communicate.

There is more than one system of signing, and you should work with the teacher or speech therapist to determine which system is best for your child. If you cannot get information about signs from them, contact the local association for the deaf.

BLISS SYMBOLS

Another means of nonverbal communication which you might consider using with your child is Bliss symbols. These symbols were designed to represent single words, groups of words, complex thoughts, and emotions. The symbols are arranged in a left-to-right progression with individual categories extending vertically. The child points to a symbol or several symbols to express herself.

If your child is physically handicapped, it is important to evaluate her seating position and hand function before using the symbols. When hand function is severely impaired, it may be necessary to use electronic aids or have the child point with her eyes.

Bliss symbols are not good for all children without speech. Talk to your child's teacher and speech therapist before deciding to use the system. More information about Bliss symbols may be obtained by writing the Blissymbolics Communication Foundation, 862 Eglinton Avenue, East Toronto, Ontario, Canada M4G2L1.

HEARING LOSS

Hearing loss has a great effect on language development. It is extremely important to find out at the earliest possible age if a child has a hearing impairment. Hearing is important because a child needs to hear speech in order to learn to produce speech.

There are different types of hearing loss. Some types of impairment may be improved by medical treatment or surgery. In other types a properly fitted hearing aid and hearing therapy can help the child. Children with less than normal levels of hearing have a chance of not developing normal language and speech.

Some signs to look for which can indicate a possible hearing loss are listed below. For a more complete list read the book by K. Horton listed at the end of this section and consult your doctor or local audiology clinic.

• a history of chronic cough, upper respiratory infections, running nose, or middle ear trouble

- the child pulling at her ears frequently
- a need for visual clues to successfully complete simple verbal tasks
- the child's failure to respond consistently to her name or to your voice
- difficulty for the child in locating the source of sound
- the child talking in an extremely loud or soft voice

If you have questions about your child's hearing, ask her teacher if she also has noticed signs of hearing loss, and ask whether or not the school will be testing the child's hearing. If the school is unable to provide the type of testing your child needs, it may be able to give you the name of an audiology clinic or a doctor who specializes in testing children with handicaps. Also consult your child's doctor for advice. If you do go to a specialist to have your child's hearing tested, have the hearing therapist at the school contact the doctor before your child's examination so she can ask the doctor to look for things which will help her work with your child. And make sure she gets a report from the doctor after the examination.

READING LIST

If you would like to learn more about communication, you might want to read the following:

Bill Wilkerson Hearing and Speech Center. *Rules of Talking.* Nashville, Tenn.: Bill Wilkerson Hearing and Speech Center Language Development Programs, 1976.

Horton, K. *Facilitating Development of Language in Young Children.* Reston, Va.: Council for Exceptional Children, Early Childhood Education Institute Series, 1977.

Kent, L. R. *Language Acquisition Program for the Severely Retarded.* Champaign, Ill.: Research Press, 1974.

Schiefelbusch, R. L., ed. *Language of the Mentally Retarded.* NICHD—Mental Research Centers Series. Baltimore: University Park Press, 1974.

Vanderheiden, G., et al. "Symbol Communication for the Mentally Handicapped." *Mental Retardation* 13 (February 1975): 34–37.

Lifting, Carrying, and Positioning

Lifting, carrying, and positioning your child are important daily activities. Because of your child's physical impairment, the way in which he is moved and the position in which he then sits or lies can affect his ability to move independently and become involved in the activities around him. Because you probably have to lift your child more often than most parents, it's important that you know how to lift and carry him correctly to prevent injury to yourself and to make it easier to move him frequently.

In the course of lifting, carrying, and positioning your child, you may notice that his body stiffens when he tries to bend or straighten his head, arms, or legs. And when you try to help him, he may not seem to be cooperating. Actually, his physical handicap is preventing him from moving in a normal way. You may hear a doctor, therapist, or teacher use the word "spasticity" to describe this tendency of your child to become stiff.

Another term you may hear is "athetosis," which is used to describe a child who shows almost continuous uncontrolled movement of the head, arms, and legs. Or you might hear the term "hypotonia" to describe a child who has little muscle strength. Like spasticity, athetosis and hypotonia prevent a child from moving, sitting, and lying in a normal way.

Your child may show all three of these characteristics of muscle movement. For instance, his arm may at times be stiff when you try to move it, and at other times you might notice that it seems to move uncontrollably.

Your child's handicap may also cause him to have poor posture. Posture is important to voluntary movement. So that your child can move voluntarily, he must be able to adapt his posture constantly before and during movement. For example, to start walking from a standing position, he must automatically transfer his weight onto one leg before taking a step. Because of his poor posture and patterns of muscle movement like spasticity and athetosis, he may have difficulty moving voluntarily.

Another type of muscle movement which you may observe in your child is the result of reflexes. Some of these reflexes are present in all young children at various ages, but they are replaced by more voluntary forms of muscle coordination as the child grows older. In many physically handicapped children, these reflexes are not replaced at the same age as in normal children, and they cause abnormal movements and make more advanced forms of movement impossible.

The way in which your child is handled and positioned should be consistent in order to decrease abnormal reflexes and abnormal patterns of muscle movement. This in turn should help him sit and lie more normally and should allow the development of more normal and basic ways of moving. Some of the basic movements which are desirable are head control, arm support, and balance.

SUPPORT AND CONTROL

When you lift, carry, or position your child, you can help decrease abnormal patterns of movement by giving consistent support at several key points on your child's body. These key points are the neck and spine, the shoulders, and the pelvic area. Because of their location on the body, these points control the movement (muscle tone) in the head, arms, and legs. For

example, suppose it is time for lunch and you look at your child in his chair. You see that his body is stiff—his back is arched, his arms are stiff and thrown out to his sides. You ask him to pick up his spoon; he seems to try but can't do it. The reason is that his physical handicap prevents him from having normal posture and movement. You can help him move more normally by giving him support at a key point. In this case you would bend his hips and give support to his shoulders. This should help his body relax and enable him to move in a more normal manner. Avoid attempts to control his whole body, but rely on giving support at key points and then ask the child for voluntary movements.

Besides giving support at key points, relaxing the child who tends to become stiff can help you get him into an appropriate position for carrying. You should avoid quick movement, as this will only make the child stiffer. And tell the child that you are going to lift him so that he is not surprised by your action.

Also, to encourage relaxation, hold your child in one of the positions illustrated for carrying, and slowly rock him by shifting your body weight from side to side. Hold him securely at key points and keep him close to your body to give him support and to avoid straining your muscles.

If your child's arms and legs are stiff, you can help him relax by laying him on his side and gathering him up into a ball by bending his hips, knees, and shoulders forward. If his legs cross, place a pillow between the knees and make sure his lower arm is not under his body.

LIFTING AND CARRYING

Control of the shoulders, head, and hips is important both before carrying and while carrying your child. Different children should be carried in different ways. Your child's teacher or therapists can give you special advice about carrying your child. However, here are some possible procedures you may want to try.

If your child, while lying down, has a tendency to stiffen and straighten his body as you lift him, try bringing him to a sitting position with his hips and knees bent before lifting. Stand in front of him, place his arms around your neck and his legs around your waist. Make sure his hips and knees remain bent by allowing his weight to rest on one of your forearms. Support the rest of his body by placing your other hand on his upper back between the shoulder blades. As he develops enough control of his head and body to balance himself, move your hand down his back and give him less support. When you place him on the chair to which he has been carried, slowly

remove your support, keeping his legs and hips bent, and maintain control at the key points until he is positioned as normally as possible in the chair.

If your child is lying in a stiff position with his chin tucked to his chest and spine rounded, move him to a sitting position before lifting. Stand behind him, reach under him and place one of your hands on his pelvic area from between his legs. Place your other arm under one of his arms and across the upper part of his body, with slight pressure against his rounded shoulders.

Your child's back will be straight and braced firmly against your chest as you lift and carry.

If your child seems to have little muscle strength, he can be carried in either of the two ways described above. Give adequate support to the key points and give no more support to his head and back than is necessary to keep him in an upright position.

There are two positions for carrying which will allow your child to see where he is going while being carried. For the first one, stand behind him and extend one arm around each side of his body, giving body support at the waist. Lift and separate his legs, keeping his hips and knees bent, and rest the child on your hip bone. One arm or two arms can be used to support his back. As your child is able to improve his control of his head and body, you will want to lessen the amount of support you give him by moving your hand farther down his back.

For the second way of carrying a child so that he is looking forward, place your arms under his arms and grasp the inside of each thigh directly above the knee, exerting slight outward pressure. Your child's back is braced against your chest, giving maximum head and body control. This position will keep the hips and knees bent.

If your child is lying down and you find it difficult to bring him to a sitting position in preparation for lifting, try rolling him to his side first. To do this, bring his arms close to his body, either at the sides or across the chest, then push simultaneously at the hips and shoulders. Gently bend the child's hips and knees, place one of your arms around his shoulders to rotate them forward and down, then roll him up to a sitting position to be lifted.

Although the actual manner in which you lift and carry your child is extremely important, the most important thing to focus on in this process is making the child more independent. Before lifting and carrying, try to think of ways the child can either move himself or try to help you while you lift him. For example, if you want to lift your child from a sitting position and he cannot get into a sitting position himself, perhaps he could roll onto his side, making it easier for you to bring him to an upright position. This also makes him more involved in the activity and therefore more independent.

Planning is important. Remember to clear your walking path before you lift. And make certain that there is nothing on the chair or surface to which you plan to take your child. If you plan to seat your child in a wheelchair, remove the tray table and lock the wheels before you lift him.

To avoid straining your muscles during lifting and carrying, keep the following suggestions in mind.

1. Kneel down as close to your child as possible so that you do not have to reach out to him when you pick him up.
2. Keep your back straight, and bend at the knees rather than at the waist, holding him close to your body as you lift.
3. As you stand, don't twist your body—you might hurt your back. Once you are standing up, turn in the direction you wish to walk by moving your feet first and letting your body follow.
4. While you are carrying your child, try not to lean to one side. When

you turn, don't twist your body. And hold your child close to you so
you won't lose your balance.

5. Do not carry your child any further than is necessary.

Just as there are correct ways to carry your child, there are some things
that should not be done when you carry him. First of all, do not hold him
under his arms so that his arms and legs dangle. This may make your child

stiff and more difficult to hold. Second, don't hold him around the waist when you carry him. His head may have a tendency to push back and his legs may become stiff, making him harder to handle.

POSITIONING

A multiply handicapped child has trouble controlling his muscles. The result may be that he becomes very stiff or, sometimes, just the opposite— very floppy. Because he cannot control his muscles, even simple things may be very hard for him to do.

He might be unable to sit up by himself in a chair. Or, when he tries to reach out for something, his movements may be awkward and jerky so that he cannot reach what he wants.

You can help your child control his muscles better through good position- ing. When his body is positioned or arranged in a certain way, he will have more control over himself and his actions.

In this section, we will describe several of the positions that you should use with your child. It's important to become familiar with these positions. You can prevent red marks, bedsores, stiffness, and other problems by changing your child's position often.

When you do position your child, keep in mind that you need to work with his whole body. That's because each muscle connects with other mus- cles and they move together. For example, if your child cannot control his head, he may also have problems sitting up. Or when your child reaches for something with his hand, he may not be able to keep his head from turning. So, even if you are trying to help him control his head, you must remember that you have to correctly position his whole body.

In the following drawings and descriptions, we will try to show several dif- ferent ways to position your child. Of course, every child is different. Your child has certain abilities and handicaps that other children do not have. And you should talk to your child's teacher, therapists, and doctor about what special positions are best for your child. But you can use the following information as a starting point.

LYING ON HIS STOMACH

The two drawings show the correct and incorrect ways to position a child on his stomach.

Using a sloping wedge or a roll under your child's chest can help him

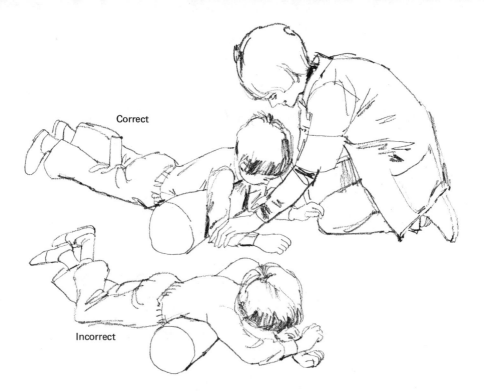

Correct

Incorrect

improve control of his head while he is lying on his stomach. Lying on a wedge can also make it easier for your child to use his hands and see what he is doing.

Lay your child on his stomach with his arms bent at the elbow and tucked under his chest with his palms down. The roll or wedge should be just high enough to hold his chest up while his forearms rest comfortably on the floor. Encourage him to keep his head centered between his arms while he is in this position. If you notice that his arms slide outward, try placing sandbags along the outsides of his arms to hold them in the correct position. If you find your child's legs closed tightly while he is on his stomach, or if they are crossed, a roll placed between his legs will keep them apart.

Sometimes, your child's hands might close up into fists while he is on his stomach. When this happens, rub the backs of his hands to see if the fingers start to relax and open. If this does not work, straighten out his arms at the elbows and bend his wrists so that the palms come toward the forearms. Your child's fingers should loosen. Then place your own hands inside his, and very gently begin to open his fingers. If they still tend to close up, even after you have helped him open them, a small toy or soft object placed in his open hands will help keep them open.

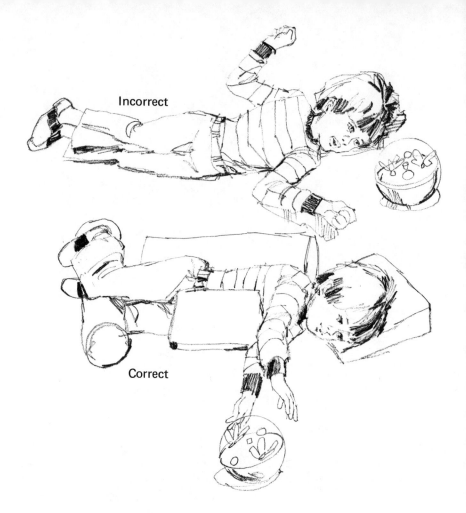

Incorrect

Correct

LYING ON HIS SIDE

The two drawings show the correct and incorrect ways to position a child on his side.

When your child is lying on his side, his head and knees should be bent. A pillow or sandbag can be placed behind his head to bend it slightly forward. And a roll can be placed between his legs to bend them and keep them relaxed. Sandbags or cushions can be placed behind his back and in front of his stomach to keep him from rolling over.

You should make sure that your child does not always lie on the same side. Changing him to the other side as often as you can will help keep him from becoming stiff and from learning to favor one side over the other.

SITTING

Because the crossed legs provide a broad base of support, sitting Indian style is a useful position for the child who seems to be in constant motion or who seems to have little muscle control. It is not, however, recommended as the only sitting position for a child who tends to have stiff joints or stiff legs.

If your child has stiff legs, a position to alternate with Indian sitting is sitting with his legs straight. This can be done when you are kneeling behind the child by bending him forward slightly at the hips and making sure he is sitting evenly on his buttocks. Grasp each leg at the knee, separating them and turning them outward at the same time. Use your body against the child's to keep his body positioned slightly forward and his hips bent. As your child's control of his body improves, you can gradually lessen the support you give his back. If your child has some body control, this procedure can be done from the front.

When you select a chair for your child to sit in, choose one which provides support for his body—especially his head, arms, and legs. As you position him in the chair, keep the following points in mind.

1. Select a chair which is the right size for your child. The chair is the right size if his bottom can comfortably be pushed all the way back to

33

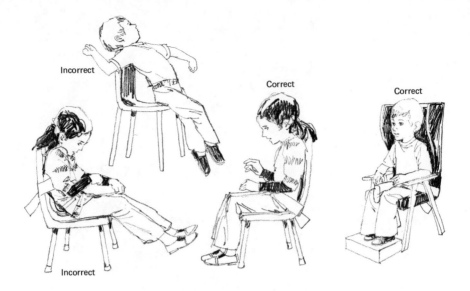

the base of the chair and his knees just bend easily over the edge of the seat. You can use pillows behind his back to make the seat fit better if it is too large.

2. When you use a belt or strap to help your child sit, it should be placed across his pelvic area below his waist. Don't put it around his waist or stomach. And don't strap your child in any tighter or more often than is absolutely necessary. Remember that you are trying to help him learn how to sit independently. And to do that he will need chances to practice sitting without a strap.

3. While your child is sitting, his arms should be relaxed, not stiff or dangling at his sides. A tray attached to the front of his chair can help. It will give his arms extra support and, at the same time, will give him a place to play with his toys.

4. If your child's legs tend to cross while he is sitting, you should use something to keep them separated. Keeping them parted at the thighs will help your child to relax, to sit back correctly in the chair, and to keep his feet flat on the floor.

5. If the chair your child sits in is too high for his feet to rest flat on the floor, you can place a box under his feet to give them the proper support. Without this support, his feet may dangle and he may become stiff and slip out of the correct position.

Your child should not spend all of his time sitting. If he stays in any one position day after day, he will become stiff and may develop sores or more serious problems. So, for a change, let him spend part of each day on the floor, supported by rolls or wedges if he needs them.

In any sitting position where the child pushes back his head, you can help by giving support at the neck. Place your forearm around his neck and shoulders, and push gently to round his shoulders slightly forward and in toward the center of his body. Sometimes a head support on the chair or a contour chair will help keep the child in this position. This should enable him to hold his head in a more normal position.

To summarize: If your child's hips and knees are usually straight and stiff, gently bend him at the hip; if his legs cross, turn them outward and gently separate them. If your child tends to stay in a curled up position, straighten his spine and neck. Work to get your child into a position which is the opposite of the abnormal one.

READING LIST

If you would like to learn more about lifting, carrying, and positioning, you might want to read the following:

Cooper, J., and Morehouse, L. E. *Assisting the Cerebral Palsied Child: Lifting and Carrying.* New York: United Cerebral Palsy Association, 1953.

Finnie, N. R. *Handling the Young Cerebral Palsied Child at Home.* New York: E. P. Dutton, 1975.

Hart, V. *Beginning with the Handicapped.* Springfield, Ill.: Charles C Thomas, 1974.

Robinault, I., ed. *Functional Aids for the Multiply Handicapped.* New York: Harper & Row, 1973.

Motor Skills

Motor skills include many things a child does—head turning, jumping, throwing a ball, even sitting. This chapter will give you information you can use to help your child improve her motor skills.

If your child is severely handicapped, her reactions to movement and being touched may be abnormal. These reaction patterns stem from the head, neck, and spine. You can help your child control these abnormal patterns by giving her support at the head, neck, and spine. These are called key points, as described in the previous chapter.

Before you work with your child on improving her motor skills, you should become familiar with correct positioning, also described in the previous chapter. Your child should be in a position which enables her to move freely and voluntarily before you ask her to learn new motor skills.

Remember that your goal is to help your child function as independently as possible. So, as she acquires new skills, begin to decrease the amount of assistance you give her. For example, parents who always provide support for their child's head may be preventing the development of necessary independent head control.

Your child's teacher or therapist can explain to you the reasons for your child's difficulties in moving; how her abnormal patterns of posture and movement affect the whole body; and how you can influence and change these reactions.

HEAD CONTROL

Head control is the basis for all our movements and activities. Whenever we move we adjust the position of our head. If your child is severely handicapped, her head control may be delayed and it may be inadequate.

You can help your child learn to control her head by using the appropri-

ate methods of handling her as well as by placing her in positions which make it easier for her to use her head independently.

In handling, your aim is to take away your support as soon as possible, remembering that when you are holding and moving the child *you* are doing the movement. You must encourage your child to move without help. She can only do so if you take away your hands at the right moment and encourage her to move by herself.

Helping your child learn to turn her head will help her develop and use

muscles that she will need to lift her head. First, help your child turn her head from one side to the other while she is lying on her stomach. Ring a bell or call her name when you are behind her to make her turn her head to see where the sound is coming from. This will also help increase her awareness of objects or activity in her environment.

If your child is able to turn her head, try to get her to lift her head straight up and hold it up while she is lying on her stomach. To help her do this, place a roll or wedge under her chest. This will usually make her more relaxed and create the best position for her to be in while she is learning to raise her head. To get her to raise her head, try to catch her eye by moving a large colorful toy, a mirror, or a noisemaker in front of her. Once she is looking at it, raise the toy so that she will have to lift her head to follow it. When your child is lying on her stomach with her head up, she can look at what is going on around her and learn from it.

There are a few important things you should know about helping your child lift her head. If she turns her head to one side as she lifts it, she should be helped to pick it straight up. Also, make sure that she holds herself up on both arms. If she doesn't pick her head up, try rubbing firmly up and down on the back of her neck. This helps some children to raise their heads.

REACHING

If your child tends to be in constant motion (athetosis), she has little difficulty in attempting to reach out, but because the movement is involuntary it may seem poorly timed and directed.

The child who tends to be stiff will be restricted in her ability to reach out. Any excitement will most likely result in making her stiffer, with her arms bending and being pressed against her body. Or she may reach out but with stiffly extended arms which are turned in at the shoulders.

Teach your child to reach out *only* after you have carefully observed her and have an idea of what positions to use to help her move independently. Start by encouraging her to reach out when you go to pick her up, and get her to hold her own arms up and forward when you wash or dress her. Gradually ask her to help you more with these activities.

While your child is lying on her stomach, encourage her to reach out and hold onto toys. Toys with handles are the best for this. For example, you might use a rattle with a large handle. Also, sponge balls or soft toys are easy to pick up and hold. At times, you should use things with your child that move easily when she touches them. For example, let her play with a ball. If she sees it move when she touches it, she may want to reach for it again. If it's fun for her, she will practice reaching more often.

You can also try using a piece of yarn with loops at each end to get your child to practice reaching. You hold one loop and your child holds the other. Gently pull the yarn toward you. By simply holding onto the other end, your child will be learning a movement that is very much like reaching.

As your child begins to reach for things by herself, you should give her chances to practice reaching in different directions. Have her reach for objects above her head, to the side of her, or far in front of her. Try to make a game out of this by using things that she likes to play with. The more pleasant the game is, the harder she will try to reach.

When you handle your child throughout the day, encourage her to become familiar with her hands. For example, when giving her her bottle, place her open hands around it. As in any new activity it is only by constant repetition that a child learns, so give her every opportunity to support herself on her hands and to grasp and release.

ROLLING

When the severely physically handicapped child attempts to roll, she has difficulty because her body may be either too floppy or too stiff. This is because of her inability to control the position of her head and her general stiffness, constant motion, or lack of muscle strength—all of which can prevent coordinated sequences of movement between her shoulders and hips.

When the child is not so severely handicapped, she will be able to begin the movement, but with varying degrees of effort according to the degree of stiffness or uncontrollable motion. Neither the beginning of the movement nor the movement itself may appear to be "normal."

When your child can perform a movement but does so abnormally, you will need to position her or give her support at a key point to minimize the abnormal movement. Whenever possible, aim not only to get the child to move, but to continue to improve the quality of her movements.

Rolling can make it possible for your child to change her own position. If she is tired of lying on her side, for example, she can roll over onto her stomach. Also, if she learns to roll very well, she will be able to move from one place to another by herself.

You can start this training by teaching your child to roll from her stomach to her back. She should begin the roll with her head and shoulders while her legs are bent only slightly. Don't let your child attempt to roll when she is curled up in a ball. This could become a bad habit which will keep her from learning the right way to roll.

You can teach her how to roll any time during the day by making rolling a part of her daily routine. For example, try to have your child roll over once before you get her out of bed each morning. However, rolling should be done in conjunction with another activity. The child should roll towards something or out of a position which is uncomfortable. This will help her learn that she can have some control over her environment and use rolling as a way of getting things she wants.

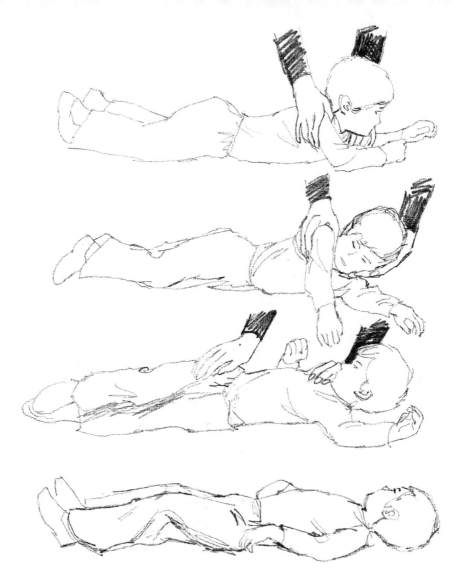

LEG MOVEMENT

Encourage your child to move her legs often. For instance, while diapering her lift both her legs in the air, bend her legs at the knees, and then straighten them. Do this several times. Or, while she is sitting in a chair, you can play a "marching" game with her, helping her to lift first her left foot and then her right foot up and down. As you move her legs, you might even say, "Left-right-left-right." Try to think of other ways to give your child practice moving her legs, like kicking a ball or pushing her feet into socks or pants while dressing.

Crawling can be harmful to the child who tends to become stiff, because pulling herself across a floor on her stomach can strengthen abnormal patterns of movement. Her chin may push downward against her chest and head lifting may become impossible. The hips will become stiff and straight and the toes pointed. Children who appear to be in constant motion often cannot crawl because they are unable to lift their heads or bear any weight on their arms. An alternative to crawling is the use of a scooter board for those children who lack good head control.

Before working on standing with your child, consult a physical or occupational therapist or a doctor. This is important for two reasons. If your child has dislocated hips, standing can further injure the joints as well as cause pain. Second, pressure on the ball of the foot can cause some children to walk abnormally.

If your child is able to stand without assistance and is able to put her hands out to catch herself when she falls, you may want to try putting her in a position to help her learn to walk. But talk to your doctor or therapist before using this position. Stand behind your child and grasp each of her arms by the elbows. Straighten and turn out her arms, pushing the shoulders up and forward. Avoid holding her under the arms and leaning her forward to encourage walking, because she will probably fall forward and try to catch herself. This may cause her legs to stiffen and then to cross.

MOBILITY

As the normal child becomes mobile in her environment through rolling, creeping, crawling, and finally walking, she learns many things. Her mobility allows her to explore and to discover social situations. Severely handicapped children seldom can acquire mobility skills independently: Even rolling is difficult for many. Thus, their environments become limited to what other persons expose them to or make possible for them.

The nature of your child's handicap and her functional abilities will determine the type of equipment which will help her develop mobility.

Walkers, scooters, crawlers, wheelchairs—either commercially available or homemade—can provide mobility. You can best select these items with the help of your physical therapist or occupational therapist. See the chapter "Special Equipment," page 93, for further information.

READING LIST

If you would like to learn more about motor skills, you might want to read the following:

Finnie, N. R. *Handling the Young Cerebral Palsied Child at Home.* New York: E. P. Dutton, 1975.

Hart, V. *Beginning with the Handicapped.* Springfield, Ill.: Charles C Thomas, 1974.

Feeding

One of the first things parents want their child to learn is how to feed himself. But eating is not a simple activity. Whether your child uses a spoon or fork or finger feeds, he must be able to hold his head up, sit up, pick up the food, bring the food to his mouth, put the food into his mouth, move it around with his tongue, chew it, and swallow it.

If your child is learning to feed himself at school, ask his teacher how she is training him and what things seem to work best. She should be able to give you advice about what you can do to help your child at home. While you are talking with her, find out how you can keep a record of his improvement as you work with him. This will let you see how well he is doing. Also, you can use the record to show the teacher what is happening at home. Let the teacher know about any things that work for you at home. Your child will benefit when you share your information.

This chapter will give you some ideas on how you can position your child so he can sit up to eat. And it gives you some hints on how to help him chew and swallow correctly. It also offers ideas about how you can train your child to feed himself. For other suggestions, talk to your child's teacher or therapists, or read some of the material listed at the end of this chapter.

POSITIONS FOR FEEDING

The first step in feeding your child is to position him correctly. The best position for feeding is a sitting position. Hold the child on your lap, or seat him in a chair, so that he is sitting up with his head slightly forward. It may be necessary to put something behind his head to keep it from pushing back. Or, you might have to hold his head so that it will not fall forward. With his head in the correct position, he will be able to chew and swallow much better.

It is not a good idea to put the food into your child's mouth when his head is tipped back. This is called "birdfeeding." Not only will birdfeeding keep him from learning how to swallow correctly, but he might take the food into his lungs rather than his stomach.

HELPING HIM TO CHEW AND SWALLOW

When you begin to help your child improve his chewing and swallowing, it may be necessary to use either pureed, semisolid, or crunchy foods. If your child does not chew, begin with puree and as his ability to chew improves, gradually thicken the food until it is semisolid. At this point it is helpful to try a crunchy food which becomes soft quickly once it is in the mouth. A potato chip is a good example. The reason for using such a food is that it is fun for the child to hear the crunch as he begins to chew and to associate this with progress he has made.

If your child has a tongue thrust, it will interfere with his chewing and will make it difficult for him to keep food in his mouth. This is caused by a reflex which pushes the tongue forward and out of the mouth. As a general rule do not try to put a spoonful of food into your child's mouth when his tongue is sticking out. Try "walking the tongue back" by using a rubber-coated spoon without food on it. Starting at the tip of the tongue, push down and back. Do this two or three times, moving toward the middle of the tongue each time. This should help the tongue move back into the mouth. As soon as you have finished, and your child's tongue is no longer sticking out, put the spoon with the food on it into his mouth. Another idea is to press down on the center of his tongue with the spoon as you put food into his mouth. You may also find that putting the spoon in at the side of his mouth instead of directly in front is helpful.

A bite reflex can make a child bite down too hard on the spoon when it is placed in his mouth. If your child seems to do this, it may help to rub his gums before feeding him. You should rub on both sides of his gums, not in the front. Metal spoons often set off the bite reflex when they hit a child's teeth. So, it may help to use a rubber-coated spoon or a small spoon which will not scrape the child's teeth.

Because your child will need to learn how to shift food back and forth inside his mouth to chew solid foods properly, try putting the food into his mouth from the side instead of the front. Watch to see if he uses his tongue to move the food for chewing. You will be able to see if he uses a sucking motion instead of his tongue by watching his lips and cheeks.

Using a technique called jaw control during feeding is a way to help your child chew, bite, and swallow more correctly. It will also help him learn to close his mouth while chewing, which will result in less food loss. When you use jaw control, you are helping him eat by controlling the movement of his jaw or lips with your fingers. Because he may take awhile to get used to this, begin by using it only for short periods of time. The drawings show you how to hold your hand for correct jaw control.

If you are sitting beside your child, put your arm around the back of his head. Then,

1. Put your middle finger under his chin.
2. Place your index finger on the front of his chin.
3. Use your thumb on the side of his cheek to control his head.

If you are sitting in front of your child,

1. Place your middle finger under his chin to help you control his jaw.
2. Put your thumb on the front of his chin, where it can help you close his lips and control his jaw.
3. Place your index finger along the side of his cheek to control his head.

While using jaw control make sure to help the child use his lips to take food off the spoon. You may have to lift the spoon slightly as you pull it out of his mouth to let the top lip scrape the food off the spoon.

It is also important for your child to use his lips properly when drinking. He should be able to close his lips on the edge of the cup so that the liquid will stay in his mouth. You can also use jaw control to help him do this, too. There should be enough liquid in the cup so that your child does not have to tip his head backward to drink it. Position his body so that his head is tipped slightly forward; this will make it easier for him to swallow. A thin liquid may be hard for him to drink. A thicker liquid, such as tomato or apricot juice or a milk shake, will not leak out of his mouth. A drinking straw is a useful aid if your child has trouble drinking directly from a cup. Drinking through a straw reduces drooling and facilitates swallowing.

Jaw control will help you teach your child how to eat and drink better while you feed him. If your child already feeds himself but does not chew or swallow properly, you may need to feed him for part of the meal using jaw control to help him learn more appropriate eating patterns. Your child's teacher and therapists can help you decide if jaw control is appropriate for your child and can help you learn to use the technique correctly.

Noise or interruptions during mealtime may make your child too excited to eat. Then it may be hard to work with him on new things like jaw control. So, when you begin to help him with his chewing or swallowing, try to feed

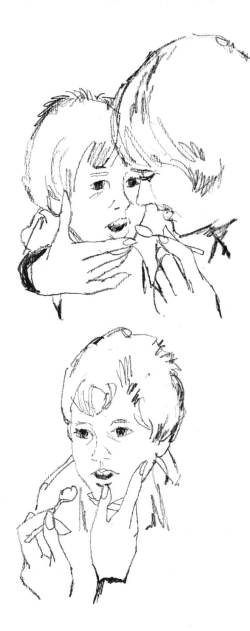

him in a quiet place. As he learns to chew and swallow and needs less help, he will probably be able to eat even when there are interruptions and some noise. If you want to feed your child away from the family because of the problems we have talked about, try feeding him a little earlier than the rest of the family. But then bring him to the table so he can enjoy being with the family at mealtime. He could have his dessert or some fruit while the others eat.

TEACHING HIM TO FEED HIMSELF

Children will usually pick up food and eat it with their fingers before they use a spoon or fork. This is called finger feeding. Teaching your child to finger feed will help him learn how much food he should put in his mouth at one time.

When you begin to teach him to finger feed, be sure that he picks up one piece of food at a time. Don't let him put a second piece of food in his mouth before he finishes chewing the first. You can begin training him to do this by putting one piece of food on his plate at a time. As he learns to eat one piece of food before reaching for another, you can put more and more food on his plate.

As your child learns to finger feed, you can begin teaching him to spoon-feed himself. To begin with, help him bring the food to his mouth by moving his hand with your own hand. As he begins to lift the spoon himself, you should give him less help. For example, instead of moving his hand with your hand, you would just move his wrist, then his arm, and then his elbow. As he starts to get better at feeding himself, show him that this makes you happy. This will reward him and will make him try harder.

Use your child's favorite foods when you begin to teach him spoon-feeding. As he gets better at it, begin to feed him more foods that are good for him, even though they may not be his favorites. To make spoon-feeding easier, try to use foods which stick to the spoon: cooked cereal, rice pudding, mashed potatoes, cream cheese, junior baby foods, desserts like mashed bananas or instant pudding, or any soft pureed foods. As his spoon-feeding improves, use thicker foods. For example, you can add oatmeal cereal or potato flakes to make the puree thicker.

READING LIST

If you would like to learn more about feeding, you might want to read the following:

Bensberg, G. J., ed. *Teaching the Mentally Retarded: A Handbook for Ward Personnel.* Atlanta: Southern Regional Education Board, 1966.

Bureau of Crippled Children. *A Helpful Guide in the Training of a Mentally Retarded Child.* Richmond, Va.: Virginia State Department of Health, 1968.

Bureau of Public Health Nutrition. *A Guide for Feeding Children with Cerebral Palsy.* California State Department of Public Health, 1966.

Finnie, N. R. *Handling the Young Cerebral Palsied Child at Home.* New York: E. P. Dutton, 1975.

Robinault, I., ed. *Functional Aids for the Multiply Handicapped.* New York: Harper & Row, 1973.

Watson, L., Jr. *How to Use Behavior Modification with Mentally Retarded and Autistic Children: Programs for Administrators, Teachers, Parents and Nurses.* Columbus, Ohio: Behavior Modification Technology, 1972.

Dressing

Before you try to teach your child how to manage her clothing, it may help to talk to her teacher or therapists. You can work with them to make sure that the way she is taught to dress at home is similar to the way she is being taught in school. This will keep her from becoming confused and will help her learn faster.

Correct positioning will help minimize the abnormal movements of your child's body while you dress her and, if she tends to be stiff, this will help keep her relaxed. If she is relaxed, it will be easier for you to dress her and easier for her to learn to dress herself. Remember that your child will try harder if you praise her. So show her that you are pleased when she tries—even if she doesn't do things just right.

In this chapter there is information on clothing you can use for your child, on ways to make dressing your child easier, and on how to help your child learn to dress herself.

CLOTHING

Try to dress your child in the same style of clothes worn by other children her age. Choose clothing that allows your child to move easily. Generally speaking, simple styles allow freedom of movement and are easy to wash and iron.

Sometimes you will have to make changes in clothes so that your child can learn to dress more easily. For example, you may need to replace small buttons with large ones when you teach her buttoning. They should be at least as big as a nickel, flat, and sewn on to stand out a little bit from the material. Since zippers can be hard to use, you may want to add a cloth loop or a metal ring to the end of a zipper to make it easier for your child to hold and pull. Use elastic waistbands instead of belts on pants and skirts. The elastic makes it easier to pull on and off the clothing.

You might also want to use Velcro tape instead of zippers, since it makes dressing much simpler. Just press both pieces of the tape together to close the clothing, and pull them apart to open it. This will give the child who isn't ready to use zippers the opportunity to dress independently. Make sure you stick the two sides of tape together before putting clothes into the washing machine. Otherwise the Velcro might snag on other clothes.

If your child wears leg braces, choose pants for her which are loose enough to fit over her braces. Sewing zippers into the inside leg seams will make the pants easier to put on. Also, it may help to line the inside of the pants with extra cloth to keep them from wearing out when they rub against her braces. One simple way of doing this is to line a pair of trousers with proper size pajama pants.

If your child uses crutches, sew pieces of cloth under the arms of shirts or blouses to keep them from wearing out. Shirts with longer shirttails will stay tucked in and help your child maintain a neat appearance.

If you have an older child who needs diapers, you will want to use large, contour-type diapers which absorb well but don't have much bulk between the legs. You can get sewing patterns for them from the United Cerebral Palsy Association, 66 East 34th Street, New York, N.Y. 10016.

DRESSING YOUR CHILD

Careful positioning and handling of your child while you dress her is important. The reason for this is to minimize the effects of any abnormal posture or patterns of movement in your child.

Some children will stiffen and become more difficult to handle when they are lying on their back then when they are in any other position. In this position they have a tendency to push the head and shoulders back, straightening and stiffening the hips and legs.

If your child has this tendency, dress her in a sitting position whenever possible. In this position she will be easier to handle and will see more of what is going on. Let her sit on the bed and lean against you, or have her sit on your lap.

If you are dressing your child while she is sitting on your lap, you should use your body to help her stay in a relaxed position. To do this, put your knees between the child's legs to hold them apart. If she pushes her body backwards, use your body to keep her head bent forward.

If your child is too heavy to hold in a sitting position, you may want to dress her lying on her side or, if she will not stiffen, lying on her back. You

can try both positions to see which one works best for her. If you place her on her back, use a pillow to raise her head and shoulders a little. This will make it easier to bring her arms forward and to bend her hips and legs.

Whatever position you dress her in, lay out your child's clothes in front of her and tell her what you are doing as you dress her. Remember to use simple phrases when you talk to her and encourage her to help you. Also, if you lay out her clothing nearby before you start to dress her, you won't have to get up once you have your child in a good dressing position.

If she becomes tense while you are dressing her, wait for her to relax before going on. Sometimes gentle rocking and rolling can help a stiff child to relax.

If you need to bend your child's arm to get her hand into a sleeve, move

her arm from the elbow rather than from the wrist. Bending her arm this way will keep it from getting stiff and will make it easier to get her hand into the sleeve.

Similarly, if you need to bend her leg to get her foot started into her pants, move her leg from the knee rather than from the ankle. This will keep her leg from getting stiff and will make it easier for both of you to put her leg into her pants.

You can put a shoe on your child's foot more easily if her leg is bent and if her foot is bent upward to help the foot relax. If your child's toes curl, you will have trouble putting her shoes on. In this case, push down on the top of the foot until her toes uncurl. If you try to pull the toes open, they may just curl more tightly.

When diapering your child, bend her legs at the knees to place the diaper under her bottom. If you try to lift both of her legs, she may become stiff and this will make it hard for you to diaper her.

TEACHING DRESSING

Always make your child an active part of the dressing process. Even the smallest effort should be encouraged. For example, if she cooperates in being positioned, that's a help. And if she is able to move her arms or legs and not resist dressing, that is also a contribution. By early encouragement, she will be used to cooperating and will be able to help herself more as she develops the motor skills for difficult dressing tasks.

Start where you are sure she has a chance of success. Since it is easier to

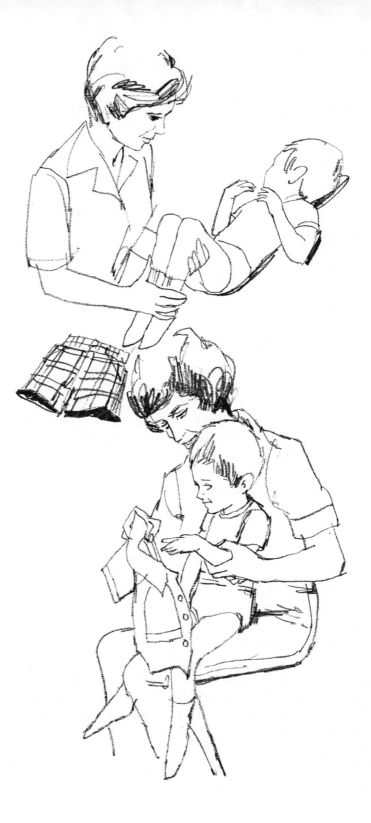

54

take things off than to put them on, begin with taking off something. This will ensure quick success and will encourage her to keep on trying.

When deciding what dressing activities are the most important to begin with, think about those which will help her to become more independent in other areas of self-care. For example, in the case of toilet training, your child will need to be able to push down and pull up her pants. You might begin your home program by having her help when you take off her pajamas in the morning or her underwear and pants in the evening. Break the activity into small steps and use brief instructions. Usually three or four words like "Pull down your pants" are enough. Try to use the same words each time so that she doesn't become confused. If she doesn't seem to understand your request at first, repeat it as you demonstrate what you want her to do. As you pull down her pants, hold her hand under yours and let her help.

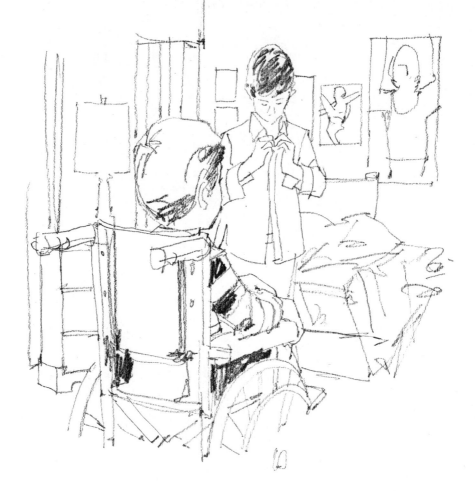

When you have removed one leg from the pants, let her pull the pants off the second leg herself. As she masters this part of the task, ask her to pull both legs out of the pants herself. Gradually lessen the amount of guidance you give her until you feel her hands begin to move independently under yours. With your help, she will learn to pull the pants off both feet first, then down from both knees and finally down from her hips. Remember to give her praise at every step and avoid scolding her when she doesn't do it just right.

Opportunities to help your child develop independence in dressing will occur daily. When she first straightens her arms into the sleeve you are holding, she is learning. When she extends her foot for the first time, she is learning. Be aware of small changes. The way her body feels as you help her provides many clues. If her fingers grasp under yours a tiny bit as you help her pull her pants down, she is making progress. Encourage her to watch

56

her brothers or sisters dress. Many children learn to dress themselves by watching others.

Don't push your child to move too fast when she is trying to dress herself. Let her try over and over again, even when she makes mistakes. Give her rewards and praise when she does something right, or at least tries. Don't take over. Give her just enough help so that she knows what you want her to do. Then let her do as much as she can by herself.

READING LIST

If you would like to learn more about dressing, you might want to read the following:

Bare, C.; Boettke, E.; and Waggoner, N. Self-help Clothing for Handicapped Children. Chicago: National Easter Seal Society for Crippled Children and Adults, 1962.

Dayan, M., et al. Communication for the Severely and Profoundly Handicapped. Denver, Colo.: Love Publishing Company, 1977.

Ferguson, W. R. Helpful Guide in the Training of the Mentally Retarded Child. Virginia State Department of Health, Bureau of Crippled Children, 1968.

Finnie, N. R. Handling the Young Cerebral Palsied Child at Home. New York: E. P. Dutton, 1975.

Robinault, I., ed. Functional Aids for the Multiply Handicapped. New York: Harper & Row, 1973.

Watson, L., Jr. Child Behavior Modification: A Manual for Teachers, Nurses and Parents. Elmsford, N.Y.: Pergamon Press, 1973.

Watson, L., Jr. How to Use Behavior Modification with Mentally Retarded and Autistic Children: Programs for Administrators, Teachers, Parents and Nurses. Columbus, Ohio: Behavior Modification Technology, 1972.

Toilet Training

Toilet training is a complex activity. A child must move to the toilet or potty-chair, manage his clothing, urinate or defecate, clean himself, flush the toilet, and wash his hands. (See also the following chapter on hygiene.) If you try to teach your child this sequence all at once or before he is ready, toilet training can be frustrating for both of you.

Your child's teacher and therapists can help you plan his toilet training program. If you work with them on the same program, it will keep him from becoming confused and he will learn more quickly.

To find out if your child is ready for training, keep a record of the number of times he wets and has bowel movements. Check him for wet or soiled pants every half hour. If he is dry for three half hours in a row on at least half the days he is checked and if he doesn't have more than two bowel movements a day, he is ready for training. If his bowel movements are not solid, you should check with his doctor to see if there is a problem.

Also note whether the child seems uncomfortable when he has wet or soiled pants. He needs to have some idea that there is a difference between having wet and dry pants before the training can be really successful. Some parents have been able to show their child the difference between wet and dry by using a doll.

Do not be disturbed if your child is not ready to be trained at the same age as other children. Severely handicapped children are often not trained as early as other children because they may not understand the training procedures well enough to benefit from them.

To begin, try using a potty-seat that will fit over the regular commode. This is preferable to a potty-chair because it is more like the commode, which is what you eventually want your child to use. Make sure that he feels secure on the seat; if he feels as if he is going to fall in, he will not be able to relax and it will be hard for him to cooperate.

If your child is not comfortable on the potty-seat, try using a potty-chair.

There are several things you can do to make sure that he is relaxed and supported on the potty-chair. It may help him to relax if you rock him slowly before putting him on the chair. If he has trouble holding his head up or balancing his body, use a potty-chair with a headrest and armrests. Also make sure that his feet are on the floor or some other support.

Even if you have to use a potty-chair for training, you should do the training in the bathroom. This way your child will connect being in the bathroom with urinating and having a bowel movement. Also, there will be fewer distractions in the bathroom than in another room of the house.

Use loosely fitting training pants during training instead of diapers. Training pants are easy to get off in a hurry, and your child needs to learn to push them down by himself as part of toilet training. Before formal toilet training begins, it would be a good idea to help your child learn to take his pants off and get them on again so that this doesn't become the focus of attention. You can begin by asking him to help you push them down and pull them up when you change his diaper and routinely undress and dress him. Put your hands over his and guide them as he pushes the pants down. At the very end of the push, remove your hands and let him finish pushing down the last inch or so. When it is time to push the pants down in the bathroom, he will already be familiar with the activity and may be able to assist you or to do it independently.

Take your child to the toilet just before you think he is going to urinate or have a bowel movement. Sometimes he may give you signs that he has to go—by making faces, crossing his legs, or wriggling. Usually, however, you'll have to guess by figuring out about what time of the day he urinates and has bowel movements. You can do this by looking at the record you have kept. So, for example, if the record shows that he usually has a bowel movement about 1:30 in the afternoon, put him on the potty about 1:20.

The idea is that your child should be on some kind of schedule. If he doesn't go at about the same time each day, you should try taking him to the toilet once every hour.

When it is time to take your child to the bathroom, use simple commands like "Go to the bathroom." Use gestures to show him what you mean. For example, point to the bathroom. Ask him to say "bathroom" or devise a gesture or other sign to represent the word "bathroom." Reward your child when he shows you in any way that he wants to go to the bathroom. Bit by bit he may learn to let you know when he has to go, or go to the bathroom by himself.

If your child is able to walk, crawl, or otherwise move about, you should try to have him get to the bathroom on his own, even from the beginning of training. However, if a struggle is required or if the process is very time-consuming, it would be better for you to help him with this step initially. For example, if he crawls but very slowly, pick him up and carry him to the door of the bathroom and let him crawl the last few feet to the toilet. As he develops better crawling speed, you can increase the distance he crawls to the toilet. Depending on the circumstances, you may decide to carry him part or all of the way. If you do decide to carry him, remember to explain to him what you are doing, and ask for his cooperation.

Then help your child remove his pants, as explained earlier, and place him on the potty-seat or -chair. Gradually increase the amount of time he sits on the potty, up to about ten minutes. Don't keep him on the seat so long that he becomes upset. And don't punish him when he isn't able to do

anything. Instead, keep taking him to the toilet until he urinates or has a bowel movement. And remember to reward him for his efforts.

When your child has an accident, change him as soon as possible. Don't let him get used to being wet or soiled. Show him again the difference between wet and dry by having him touch his wet pants and having him help you change them. Gently draw his attention to the fact that he eliminated in the wrong place. But don't scold him severely or he may become afraid of the bathroom.

Keep a chart so that you know how the training is progressing. The chart should show when he urinates or has bowel movements in the potty or toilet and when he has accidents. A chart will also help his teacher see how training is going at home. Show it to her when you are discussing his training at your parent conference, and send her frequent reports of his progress.

READING LIST

If you would like to learn more about toilet training, you might want to read the following:

Bensberg, G. J., ed. *Teaching the Mentally Retarded: A Handbook for Ward Personnel.* Atlanta, Ga.: Southern Regional Education Board, 1966.

Finnie, N. R. *Handling the Young Cerebral Palsied Child at Home.* New York: E. P. Dutton, 1975.

Foxx, R. M., and Azrin, N. H. *Toilet Training the Retarded: A Rapid Program for Day and Nighttime Independent Toileting.* Champaign, Ill.: Research Press, 1974.

Robinault, I., ed. *Functional Aids for the Multiply Handicapped.* New York: Harper & Row, 1973.

Watson, L., Jr. *How to Use Behavior Modification with Mentally Retarded and Autistic Children: Programs for Administrators, Teachers, Parents and Nurses.* Columbus, Ohio: Behavior Modification Technology, 1972.

Hygiene

Hygiene deals with keeping the body clean and healthy through such things as hair and skin care, dental care, and washing. Of course, it's important to take care of your child's body. But it's also important to give her the chance to learn to care for herself.

If you do things regularly, your child will begin to learn what to expect at different times during the day. For example, try always to brush her teeth after breakfast or comb her hair every morning. And on days that you give your child a bath, try to do it at the same time of the day. As she gets to know when things are going to happen, she will be more relaxed when they are done.

Try to help your child with these activities at a time when you won't be rushed. This will give you enough time to give her the help she needs, and to let her try some things on her own.

When you begin training your child to do something, be sure you help her through each step. Try to perform each task in approximately the same order each time. This will help your child learn faster. Most children learn these steps in order simply by watching others, so create situations to let your child watch others perform the task she is learning. You might try showing her the task before you ask her to do it so that she has a chance to learn by watching. She will also need to practice the task many times before she will understand the sequence.

For each step, tell her what you want her to do by using simple sentences like "Wash your hands" or "Dry your face." Gradually, help her less and less so that she can begin to learn to do these things by herself. Remember to reward her when she does what you ask, or when she tries to help herself.

WASHING

It is important to keep your child clean and help her learn the importance of cleanliness. It can be difficult to bathe a handicapped child and difficult for the child to learn to bathe herself. But keeping her clean will help ensure that she is greeted positively by others.

Washing is a fairly complex task, and it will help you to teach your child if you think of the task as several separate skills which she must learn to link together. For example, to wash her hands, she must find the sink and faucets, then turn on the faucets, mix hot and cold water, wet her hands, find the soap, rub the soap between her hands, replace the soap, rinse her hands, find the faucets, turn them off, find the towel, dry her hands, and replace the towel on the rack.

If your child can stand or sit at the sink to wash her hands, place your hands over hers and help her go through the steps for washing. Be sure she is paying attention to what is being done. As one hand turns on the water, be sure the other hand is under the faucet to feel the water as it begins to come out. When she shows that she can do any part of the washing herself, let her try. And reward her for trying.

If your child is not tall enough to reach the sink, keep a wooden box under the sink for her to stand on. You can also sew curtain rings on washcloths and towels and install hooks to hang them on. This is easier for some children than putting a towel on a slippery towel rack. Another idea is to tie the soap to the sink with a string. This will keep it from falling on the floor or into the sink.

Your child may often hold her hands in fists because of her physical handicap. This can make it hard to wash her hands. Here are some things that might help you to open your child's hands for washing:

1. Make sure your child is relaxed.
2. Stroke downward on top of her hand with a washcloth.
3. Bend your child's wrist so that the palm comes down toward her forearm.
4. If her hand still won't open, straighten out her fingers one by one, beginning with the little finger.

When bathing your child, wash her in a bathtub whenever possible. Not only can you get her cleaner in a tub, but bathing can be fun for her. If it is hard for your child to sit up in a bathtub, you might want to use a chair or special seat in the tub. This can make bathing her easier and safer. A small lawn chair with short legs and a back that can move up and down can be used. This type of chair will give support to your child's head and can be adjusted to suit her needs. If you use the chair, make sure it has rubber tips on the legs to keep it from slipping. A tub seat that fits into the tub can be made from a plastic washbasket. For more information about tub seats, see the chapter on "Special Equipment," page 93.

DENTAL CARE

Regular dental care is important for your handicapped child, as it is for any child. Cavities can lead to missing teeth. And a child with missing teeth can have problems eating and speaking correctly. Everyday home care and regular dental checkups can help prevent cavities.

You should take your child to the dentist for a checkup about every four months. The dentist can show you how to brush and use dental floss properly to clean your child's teeth. He can also tell you about good eating habits. For example, he will probably tell you that you should not give your child too many sweet things to eat because they can be bad for her teeth.

Begin to brush your child's teeth slowly and calmly, without forcing her. This can help her learn to like brushing and prevent her from resisting or fearing the toothbrush. If possible, your child's teeth should be brushed after every meal. It is best to brush from side to side, using short up and down movements. Also be sure to gently brush the gums. A small toothbrush with soft bristles is easier to move around inside your child's mouth, especially if she gags or has a tongue thrust. Be willing to accept small amounts of progress. If she lets you put the toothbrush in her mouth, this may be progress. If she refuses to open her mouth, start with trying to get her to open a small amount. Often a small taste of honey or other favorite food on your finger will encourage her to open her mouth. Next you might put a taste of this on the toothbrush and, once she is accustomed to the brush being in her mouth, switch to toothpaste.

Remember to reward her. Looking in the mirror after brushing and talking about her pretty shiny teeth is often rewarding. She will also benefit from watching others brush their teeth—perhaps Dad or big brother will help here.

If your child has trouble holding the toothbrush, add an elastic strap for her to put her hand through, or build up the handle of the brush to make it easier to hold. If your child's gums are very tender because of the medicine she is taking, she may not be able to use a toothbrush at all. You might want to use a Toothette instead of a brush. See the chapter on special equipment for more information.

SKIN CARE

A child who has to stay in bed for a long time may develop bed sores. To stop this from happening, change her position often and keep her bed dry. If your child wears braces, she may get red marks on her skin. This means that the braces do not fit. You should see your doctor about this as soon as possible.

Use a nongreasy lotion to keep your child's skin soft. Also use a nongreasy lip moistener, especially in cold weather.

HAIR CARE

Your child's hair should be washed at least once a week and cut often. Keep bangs trimmed above the eyebrows. You want to be sure that her hair is short enough to keep it out of her eyes.

Let her help comb her hair. Even if she doesn't do it just right at first, she will improve with help. Try a large comb or brush with a thick handle; this may be easier for her to use.

Always comb her hair before taking her out. She will learn to associate this experience with something important.

READING LIST

If you would like to learn more about hygiene, you might want to read the following:

Finnie, N. R. *Handling the Young Cerebral Palsied Child at Home.* New York: E. P. Dutton, 1975.

Robinault, I., ed. *Functional Aids for the Multiply Handicapped.* New York: Harper & Row, 1973.

Play and Recreation

With all the specialized kinds of help and care severely handicapped children need, it is easy to forget that they are children (or youths) and that they have much the same needs for play and recreation as other children. It is also natural that you, as a parent, because of the great demands your severely handicapped child makes upon you, tend to neglect this particular need. After all, how much can a parent be expected to do—even when you love and care for your child a great deal? And besides, most parents are used to their children playing on their own—particularly as they get older.

What one often sees, then, is the severely handicapped child parked in front of the television set and left there to watch program after program, even if he is not interested or cannot understand them. This is the easiest way for parents to try to "amuse" their handicapped children. But severely handicapped children need help in play and recreation just as much as they need it in learning how to eat, dress, and move about. And you, as a parent, can give this help without any great difficulty.

First of all, remember that most children like company. And for severely handicapped children in particular, being around other people is usually something that makes them very happy. So, whenever possible, include your child in a group. It may be with other children, or it may be with adults. Your handicapped child may not be able to do much more than just watch. But that can be fun, too! Even watching television can be something special when done in the company of others! Or have your child placed somewhere so that he can watch other children play—on your lawn or, if he must remain indoors, by a window, or on a playground. Nor should you forget that taking trips and going places is as much fun for the severely handicapped child as it is for other children or for you yourself. You don't have to take him everywhere. But don't make it a habit to leave him home all the time either.

Be sure you explain to and acquaint neighborhood children and parents with your very special child. Invite other children over, introduce your child, and get a little hand-shaking going. Have them watch a special television show together, or bring in a game your child can watch, like ring toss. Don't push too hard, but nourish the relationships and friendships that will result. In other words, try to remove the mystery of this "different" child so that the neighbor goes home feeling, "He likes me. I think I can like him too."

It is hard to expect other children who don't have serious problems to want to take time to play with a child who can't do the same things they do. But chances are that a neighbor's child, and certainly your own children, will be willing to take at least a little time with someone who needs special help. Why don't you try asking them? Or perhaps you can hire a young babysitter, of about the same age, who will talk with your child, watch television with him, or even play simple games with him.

Which brings us to games. It is easy to overlook how many things there are that your child can do which will give him pleasure and help teach him no matter how much trouble he may have performing other activities. He can sit on a floor and have a ball rolled to him; perhaps he can roll it back. He can have a cloth ball thrown to him which will stick to a special Velcro cloth sewn on his clothes; if the ball is very soft he might even be able to catch it by himself. He can get a lot of excitement from a pinball game which he shoots by himself or with help from you. There is a variety of sounds and sights in these kinds of games, and he will come to feel that he can make things happen even if he has trouble controlling his arms and hands.

Some of the new electronic games that you can hook up to your television are definitely worth considering. Almost anyone can play these, and they can be fun for you as well as your severely handicapped child when you play together.

Years ago it might have been hard for a severely handicapped child to use phonograph records to listen to songs or stories. Now there are cassette tape recorders that almost anyone can make stop and go. You can buy song and story tapes for these, or make your own from records. You should be able to arrange a number of ways for your child to use these tape recorders, even though his handicap might make it impossible with an ordinary tape recorder. Being able to work his very own tape machine should make him happy.

Parents are sometimes afraid to take chances with their multiply or severely handicapped child. But he is probably much better able to "take it" than you think. So you may be able to place him on a seesaw or a swing, even a merry-go-round (with some help) and give him rides just like all the other kids! Check with your doctor to see if this is feasible. Certainly one place where you can expect him to have fun is in a pool. It doesn't matter if

he can't swim. He can have all sorts of fun, once he gets over being scared, by being in the water even if he is handicapped. Some local YMCAs have handicapped swim programs. If they don't, try to get them to start one.

Almost all children love pets. While your child may not be able to do all the things with a dog or cat that other children do, he can still enjoy being around a pet, touching it, hearing a purr or bark, and watching the animal run around. And don't forget how much fun a bird or an aquarium can be. They don't have to be expensive to give a lot of pleasure and fun. It's much better to have your child involved with these than looking at television all the time.

One important thing about keeping your child happy: You have to be happy, too! If you want to play some games with him and you are tired or upset, that won't do him much good. Put the games off for another time. Or if you get impatient easily, set a certain amount of time to play with him and then stop. It's better to play for a short period of time when you don't feel upset than to put in hours when you don't really want to. If you are really unhappy, your child will probably know it and his play time will be spoiled.

So think about what you can manage with him, and don't make play into work for both of you.

Another thing too: There are now more and more ways and places to get your severely handicapped child involved in activities which are fun and which can take some of the work off your shoulders. Some of the agencies listed in Part III of this book can help you find a babysitter or a special place for recreation for your child. There are, for example, many camps for children who have physical problems, some with day camping, some with overnight camping. They really can be great fun for your child, teach him many skills, and give you a chance to do things you might not otherwise have a chance to do.

Finally, don't forget to ask your child's teacher or therapist for ideas about play and recreation for your child. They are experts, after all, and they will be able to give you all sorts of special ways in which you can help your child have fun. They know your child's needs in very special ways and will want to help. So don't be afraid to ask them how to help your severely handicapped child get the most out of play and recreation.

READING LIST

If you want to learn more about play and recreation for the handicapped, you might consult the following:

Buist, C. A., and Schulman, J. L. *Toys and Games for Educationally Handicapped Children.* Springfield, Ill.: Charles C Thomas, 1976.

Carlson, B. W., and Ginglend, D. R. *Play Activities for the Retarded Child.* Nashville, Tenn.: Abingdon Press, 1961.

Molloy, J. S. *Trainable Children.* New York: Thomas Y. Crowell, 1972.

Stepping Stones: Toys to Share with Handicapped Children. Albany, N.Y.: The State University of New York (55 Elk Street, Albany, N.Y. 12234), 1976.

Family Concerns

THE REST OF THE FAMILY

What we are going to say now is obvious to you. But it has to be said again. There are other people in the family besides your severely handicapped child. This is easy to forget when her needs seem so great, she requires so much attention, and you want to help her so much.

But what can happen, and what so often does happen, is that the child may take up so much of the family's time and energy that everyone else in the family begins to suffer. And in time your severely handicapped child will suffer too if things go wrong for the rest of the family.

A husband may feel (not without reason) neglected by his wife because of all the work she has to do to help a severely handicapped child develop and improve. It is important for the wife not to become solely the "mother of a handicapped child," focusing all of her energy on caring for this child. Or the wife may feel that her husband doesn't help her with the child as much as he should. Or perhaps both mother and father were working parents who come home from a long day's work to find that their real day's work is just beginning because of that child who requires so much love, so much attention—when all they would prefer to do is rest, watch television, or read.

It often happens that parents will neglect the other children in the family because their severely handicapped child needs so much from them. Even the best of children can become jealous or resentful if their parents don't pay attention to them. And although they may know that their brother or sister needs special care, this doesn't necessarily make it any better for them when their needs are overlooked. What we are trying to say is that you, as parents, are going to have to make as complete and normal a life for yourselves and the other children in your family as you can. At times this will mean that you cannot do everything you want for your handicapped child. Although it is important to include her in all family activities, it is equally im-

73

portant that she doesn't become the center of attention of these activities. You may have to make a special effort at times to ensure that the other children receive most of your attention when you are planning or carrying out a family project.

You may feel uncomfortable or guilty when your handicapped child's needs don't seem to come before those of other family members. But, in the long run, making the care of your handicapped child fit into the normal family routines will produce a more relaxed and comfortable feeling for everyone.

Along these lines, it is important for you and other members of the family to feel that getting frustrated or angry with the handicapped child is an acceptable and normal occurrence. All families have arguments and difficult moments. And your family will probably have more than most because you have a handicapped child. There are times when we all experience anger toward the ones we love, and your handicapped child should not be exempt from experiencing this part of the full range of human emotions.

The relationship between the husband and wife (the leaders of the family)—and the way they as a unit face the problem of rearing a handicapped child—greatly affects the attitudes and behavior of the other children. When parents harbor resentments, children feel this tension and express their anger or anxiety by behaving badly and demanding more attention.

If you find yourself in this situation try to sit down and work out some ways to make time for the things that you want to do. Talk about the way you feel and try to find solutions. Sometimes if both parents plan to spend time away from the family and do something special together, the situation improves. Certain organizations provide respite care, meaning they take your handicapped child for a week or sometimes more to allow you some time away from the child. Under certain circumstances, it is possible to get financial aid for the cost of this care. Contact your local mental health agency for information about respite care.

Many communities have mother's helpers who are specially trained to care for handicapped individuals. Or there may be a university nearby which has a training program in special education where you can locate students with special training to come to your home and care for the child. You might also consider sending your child to day or overnight camp. She will enjoy the change of pace and being with other children.

But most important, if this situation persists seek professional help from your local mental health center. There should be people there who can help you plan ways to have time for yourselves and to help you solve the problems you and your family are facing. They know you might have special problems because there is a handicapped child in the family. And they know that there is nothing unusual about needing some extra help to work out your difficulties.

SEX AND YOUR CHILD

Parents of a severely handicapped child may find sex to be a very difficult subject to handle as their child approaches adolescence. There are a number of reasons for this. First, these parents may still think of their child as being younger than she really is. In part this is because she is still so dependent upon them and upon other adults.

Also, some parents think and act as if their child's handicap should somehow take away her sexual urges and interests. While this may be true for some severely handicapped individuals, it is surely not true for all. But if a parent believes the child should not have sexual feelings, he or she may become upset when the child expresses interest in sex even though such an interest is perfectly normal.

Dr. Sol Gordon, author of *Sexual Rights for the People Who Happen to Be Handicapped,* feels that it is important to think of sex as something that encompasses all areas that have to do with human sexuality, including attitudes, feelings, behavior, and the way we relate to ourselves and others. He points out the most pleasant physical contact is related to sex. This is true even of the youngest of babies. Parents stroke, kiss, and cuddle them, and they respond with affection. An infant is learning through these experiences even though she does not yet talk. She will use this early learning later in life. What she learns about love, affection, and physical contact will affect her sexual attitudes and behavior when she reaches puberty. He emphasizes that handicapped children must be handled with patience and understanding.

For more information, we suggest you get in touch with the Sex Information and Education Council of the United States. They have a variety of written material and films on sexual maturation and sexuality and the handicapped person. If you are interested, write SIECUS, 137–155 North Franklin St., Hempstead, N.Y. 11550.

There are also people and places closer to home that you might want to try. One of the first ought to be your family doctor. Talk to him. The school your child attends (or her teacher) should be able to give you good advice about sex education in general and about any concerns or problems you might be experiencing with your child. Your Mental Health/Mental Retardation Unit is another place to turn to for advice on such matters. Your priest, minister, or rabbi are others with whom you might want to talk.

People and organizations such as those we have suggested above may not always be able to give you all of the answers you need. And they will sometimes give you advice that you will not agree with. But at least they will help you begin to deal with your concerns. And so we recommend them to you.

Again, try to remember that your child is growing up. As she gets older, she will normally develop sexual interests. Your awareness of this is the first step in helping her through any problems that might result.

READING LIST

For further reading on the concerns of the rest of the family, you might consult

Paterson, G. W. *Helping Your Handicapped Child.* Minneapolis: Augsburg Publishing House, 1975.

You may find useful advice regarding sex and your handicapped child in these references:

Gendel, E. S. *Sex Education of the Mentally Retarded Child in the Home.* Arlington, Texas: National Association for Retarded Citizens, 1976.

Gordon, S. *Sexual Rights for the People Who Happen to Be Handicapped.* Syracuse, New York: Center on Human Policy, Syracuse University Division of Special Education and Rehabilitation, 1974.

SIECUS. *Bibliography on Sex Education.* Hempstead, N.Y.: SIECUS (137–155 North Franklin Street, Hempstead, N.Y. 11550).

Siegel, E. *The Exceptional Child Grows Up.* New York: E. P. Dutton, 1974.

PART III

How to Find Help for Your Child—Services, Equipment, and Information

It is difficult to be a parent of a severely handicapped child. The child makes demands upon you and your family in an ongoing, perhaps increasing, way.

Still, many parents do not take advantage of all the services that can make life easier and better for them, their families, and their severely handicapped children. A few years ago, very few of these services were available. Today, while there still may not be enough, things are very much better than before. Today you can call people for advice on solving family problems, financial help, special services, or simply their understanding of the tremendous job you and the rest of your family have before you.

Take advantage of these people and these agencies. Some addresses to write and some services to look for are given in this section of the book. But you can always find out the latest and most appropriate services available to you and your child if you call your local Mental Health/Mental Retardation Unit. People there can also tell you how to get financial help. For example, did you know that in some cases financial help is provided for handicapped children through social security?

A good source to contact, if you have trouble locating parent groups concerned with your child's handicap, is Closer Look (the National Information Center for the Handicapped), Box 1492, Washington, D.C. 20013. They can send you all kinds of information on a variety of subjects.

Services and sources of other help change frequently. And the only way to find out what kind of help you can get for yourself and your child is by asking. Everyone, regardless of his income, should look into these things.

You may also need special equipment in your home. Or you might need to find out about wills and trusts. In Part III we offer suggestions about where to go and what to do in these cases. This information should save you time, trouble, and expense. And it will help you give your child the care he needs.

Special Services and Agencies

In order to help you seek out the resources you need to care for your child, we present them here in the order of their closeness to you, beginning with the family doctor. Each service is described to show how it can serve you.

Most of this chapter is devoted to national organizations which aid the severely handicapped. They are arranged alphabetically with a brief statement of each organization's purpose and a list of the services it offers.

THE FAMILY DOCTOR

Many doctors keep lists of hospital clinics and community agencies in the local area. Or, if there are no special clinics or agencies in your area, your doctor may recommend visits to various specialists. If so, he will have particular people in mind to send you to. Your family doctor is the first place to begin when you're looking for other services for your handicapped child.

VISITING NURSE SERVICES

A registered nurse who follows orders given by a doctor and performs duties of sick care at your home is often called a visiting nurse. Generally, the doctor makes the first request for nursing services of this kind. A visiting nurse association is usually a community-based group supported by contributions from local fund-raising organizations. You can find the address and phone number of your local visiting nurse association in the telephone directory. But check with your doctor first if you think you need this service.

HOMEMAKER-HOME HEALTH AIDES

These individuals can help you in times of stress. They are professionally trained and supervised women skilled in homemaking, child care, and in the care of the chronically ill. Good sources of information about homemaker services are your local United Fund or community planning council, and the public health, welfare, or mental health departments. This is not a free service and can be costly, so check the price before making any definite arrangements.

SPECIALIZED CENTERS OR CLINICS

Most large hospitals have outpatient clinics which specialize in various kinds of problems: pediatric, psychiatric, orthopedic care, for instance. Your doctor will know of these clinics. Families are usually charged for such services according to their incomes.

LOCAL HEALTH DEPARTMENT

Your local health department should know of virtually every medical and social service available in your community. In most instances it will coordinate case-finding (or identification of the handicapped), diagnosis, treatment, rehabilitative services, and follow-up care.

COMMUNITY COUNCILS

Another good source for locating special agencies is the community council of the United Fund, found in most large cities and counties. The community coordinating agency will not itself serve the child, but will provide a listing of all the service agencies in the surrounding area.

RELIGION-AFFILIATED SERVICES

The largest of such institutions and agencies are the Federation of Jewish Philanthropies, the Federation of Protestant Welfare Agencies, and the Catholic Charities. Each offers a network of health and welfare programs—a range of direct family, community, and youth activities, as well as youth guidance services.

STATE DEPARTMENTS

States organize their health and welfare services into departments or bureaus. In your state it may be the Department of Social Welfare, the Department of Mental Health, the Bureau of Children's Services, etc. Any of these should be able to give you information about, or refer you to, the particular state-supported services you need. In some cases a state agency will make the initial contact for you. The main offices of state departments are generally located in the state capital. See your local telephone directory for regional offices.

THE FEDERAL GOVERNMENT

The federal government handles special concerns about children and their problems through the Children's Bureau, which is part of the Department of Health, Education, and Welfare in Washington, D.C. The Children's Bureau publishes numerous pamphlets and booklets on children's problems and provides lists of specialized services. Military personnel and their families can obtain information on programs, agencies, and facilities for the handicapped in their community from the Office of the Surgeon General, Denver, Colorado.

NATIONAL ORGANIZATIONS

A great variety of national groups exists to aid parents, teachers, children, and practitioners in dealing with specific handicaps. These organizations, some with local chapters, range in function from the most far-reaching concern dealing with all kinds of handicaps to very specific activities focusing on rare diseases. We have listed below the national organizations that should be most generally applicable to the severely handicapped. The list is certainly not exhaustive; its aim is to cover the major resources you will find valuable for your child. For each organization we have provided pertinent data and summarized the services provided; an asterisk indicates that a service is offered only in some divisions or local chapters.

The Alexander Graham Bell Association for the Deaf, Inc.
The Volta Bureau
1537 35th Street, NW
Washington, D.C. 20007

This is an information center on deafness, with a complete list of preschool and other programs for the deaf. This center has an extensive library on deafness, as well as educational programs for parents of deaf children. It maintains no clinics or treatment centers, but refers those who inquire to the appropriate clinic, treatment center, or school. Various local parents' groups, which are affiliates of the International Parents' Organization, offer opportunities for parents to discuss their problems.

Services:
  Local chapters
  Parent meetings*
  Special literature
  Referral
  Research

American Association for the Education of the Severely/Profoundly Handicapped
1600 West Armory Way
Seattle, Wash. 98119

This national organization has a membership which includes teachers,
parents, therapists, and others concerned with services and education for
persons with severe handicaps. It is dedicated to research, personnel training, and service delivery in all aspects of education for severely handicapped
citizens.

Services:
  Special literature
  Research

American Dental Association
211 East Chicago Avenue
Chicago, Ill. 60611

This national organization operates as a referral agency for names of den-
tists, societies, and inquiries. Some local and state chapters have emergency
treatment centers. All provide information and publications. The association
will answer inquiries and refer you to the appropriate dentist, dental clinic,
local treatment center, or society. Contact your local chapter.

Services:
  Local chapters
  Special literature
  Films
  Referral
  Evaluation*
  Clinical services*
  Direct services to children*

American Foundation for the Blind, Inc.
15 West 16th Street
New York, N.Y. 10011

This private, nonprofit agency provides consultation to agencies, groups, and individuals interested in services for the blind. Although nationwide in scope, the foundation is not a direct-service agency. It will answer all inquiries and give you information on local agencies that can provide you with the best assistance.

Services:
Special literature
Films
Referral
Research

Association of University Affiliated Facilities
Suite 908
1100 17th Street, NW
Washington, D.C. 20036

The university affiliated facilities offer services to children and adults with mental retardation and other developmental and learning disabilities—including cerebral palsy, epilepsy, and autism. Services offered by each of these facilities vary. Usually, however, they provide diagnosis, evaluation, and educational planning, as well as referral to specialized educational and treatment resources. University affiliated facilities are funded primarily through the U.S. Department of Health, Education, and Welfare. For information about facilities in your area, write to the above address.

Services:
Local chapters
Parent meetings*
Special literature
Films*
Referral*
Evaluation*
Clinical services*
Public educational program*
Direct services to children*
Counseling*
Recreation*
Vocational*
Research*

Closer Look (the National Information Center for the Handicapped)
Box 1492
Washington, D.C. 20013

The aim of Closer Look is to provide practical advice on how to find educational programs and other kinds of special services for disadvantaged or handicapped children. Among its free brochures are lists of special education officials and consultants in each state, parent organizations, vocational schools, information about laws and legal rights affecting handicapped children, and a newsletter. Closer Look operates under the Department of Health, Education, and Welfare's Bureau of Education for the Handicapped. The staff will respond with an information packet that includes background pamphlets, suggestions or steps to take to locate services, facts you should know about laws affecting the handicapped, lists of helpful organizations, and suggested reading.

Services:
    Special literature
    Films
    Public educational program

The Council for Exceptional Children
1920 Association Drive
Reston, Va. 22091

With more than 67,000 members, CEC is the largest association of professional and lay persons devoted to advancing the education of all exceptional children and youth—both gifted and handicapped—in the United States and Canada. Twelve specially focused divisions provide special services, while 50 state federations and more than 940 local chapters respond to a variety of parent concerns. The council publishes four periodicals and many books, monographs, bibliographies, and media packages. It has a number of other information services and special activities which may be of interest to parents. Write to the national headquarters for complete information.

Services:
    Local chapters
    Parent meetings
    Special literature
    Films
    Referral*
    Evaluation*

Public educational program
Counseling*
Recreation*
Vocational*
Research

Epilepsy Foundation of America
1828 L Street, NW
Washington, D.C. 20036

The foundation establishes, develops, maintains, and conducts a variety of clinics, schools, camps, and other facilities for the care, treatment, education, and training of persons with epilepsy. It also promotes, supports, and conducts research into the causes and treatment of epilepsy. You can obtain free information on subjects relating to epilepsy by writing to the above address. Ask for information on the following categories: legal information, education, family information, insurance, employment, electroencephalography, or the name of the nearest chapter.

Services:
    Local chapters
    Parent meetings*
    Special literature
    Films
    Referral
    Evaluation*
    Clinical services*
    Public educational program
    Direct services to children*
    Counseling*
    Research

National Association for Retarded Citizens
2709 Avenue E East
P.O. Box 6109
Arlington, Tex. 76011

The national headquarters can send you helpful information about diagnosis, preschool programs, special education, job training, housing, or social and recreational activities for a retarded person. We urge you to write to their regional and state associations for information about special programs in your own area. Local chapters run programs such as nurseries, sheltered workshops, and recreation. They also provide counseling services for retarded children and their families. NARC, active on both state and national levels, is an important advocacy organization for retarded citizens.

Services:
  Local chapters
  Parent meetings*
  Special literature
  Films
  Referral*
  Evaluation*
  Clinical services*
  Public educational program
  Direct services to children*
  Counseling*
  Recreation*
  Vocational*
  Research

National Easter Seal Society for Crippled Children and Adults
2023 West Ogden Avenue
Chicago, Ill. 60612

Easter Seal centers will treat people disabled due to any cause. They adapt their services to specific community needs and administer their programs through rehabilitation and treatment centers, sheltered workshops, home employment services, resident and day camps, hospitals, mobile and home therapy units. Qualified professionals, working under medical direction, provide treatment.

Services:
  Local chapters
  Parent meetings*
  Special literature
  Films
  Referral
  Evaluation*
  Clinical services*
  Public educational program
  Direct services to children*
  Counseling*

Recreation*
Vocational*
Research

The National Foundation/March of Dimes
Public Education Department
P.O. Box 2000
White Plains, N.Y. 10602

The foundation is concerned with the prevention and treatment of birth defects and is organized into local chapters throughout the United States. Chapters have information on the nearest March of Dimes medical service program and will give you a list of genetic counseling services.

Services:
Local chapters
Parent meetings*
Special literature
Films
Referral
Evaluation*
Clinical services*
Public educational program*
Counseling
Research

National Genetics Foundation
250 West 57th Street
New York, N.Y. 10019

This national office supports basic and clinical research in genetics. It makes referrals for individuals or through physicians to its genetic counseling and treatment centers throughout the country.

Services:
Special literature
Referral
Public educational program
Counseling
Research

National Society for the Prevention of Blindness, Inc.
79 Madison Avenue
New York, N.Y. 10016

The society has local chapters in many states. The national society and the state chapters all carry out programs of service, education, and research on the prevention of blindness.

Services:
Local chapters
Special literature
Films
Referral
Evaluation*
Public educational program
Research

President's Committee on Mental Retardation
Washington, D.C. 20201

This is a clearinghouse for information on mental retardation services across the country. The committee publishes many pamphlets on mental retardation and has an extensive public education program.

Services:
Special literature
Films
Public educational program

Social Security Administration
Baltimore, Md. 21235

Contact this office for information about social security benefits for the handicapped. Specific questions are generally handled by local district offices, listed in all telephone directories under the heading, "United States Government, Department of Health, Education, and Welfare."

Services:
Local chapters
Special literature

United Cerebral Palsy Association, Inc.
66 East 34th Street
New York, N.Y. 10016

The national association provides guidance and services to local chapters throughout the United States. Local services include parent education, educational materials, speech therapy, preschool classes, day-care centers, social programs, recreation, psychological counseling, dental care, sheltered workshops, home services, vocational guidance, occupational and physical therapy, and medical and nursing care.

Services:
Local chapters
Parent meetings*
Special literature
Films
Referral*
Evaluation*
Clinical services*
Public educational program
Direct services to children*
Counseling*
Recreation*
Vocational*
Research

Special Equipment

The kind of special furniture and equipment that you read about in other parts of this guide—from wheelchairs to rubber-coated spoons—can be used to help your child at home and at school.

Since some of this equipment costs a lot, this section has money-saving ideas for you. It suggests ways to make some of the equipment yourself. And it also tells you about things you might have to buy and about where you can buy them.

Remember to work with your child's school when you plan to make or buy special equipment for your child. The school needs the same type of equipment that you do and can give you advice about it. If you have special equipment at home that helps your child, you should let his teacher know. She might want to try to use it at school.

Also check with other parents to see if they have slightly used items they would be willing to sell or lend.

SUPPORTS FOR SITTING AND LYING

Many of the things that you use to help keep your child in the correct position when he is sitting or lying can be made at home.

Sandbags are especially good for keeping your child's body in the right position. You can make one by filling a heavy-duty bag with sand and closing it tightly with strong cord or tape. You might want to try covering the bag with terrycloth so that it will not stick to your child's skin. If you use a cloth cover, it should have snaps so that it can be taken off and washed.

A *roll* can be made by rolling up a sheet of foam rubber. For extra strength, you can use a cardboard mailing tube as a core. The roll is then held together with tape or rubber bands. Rolls can also be covered with a cloth cover. Foam rubber can be bought in sporting goods, department

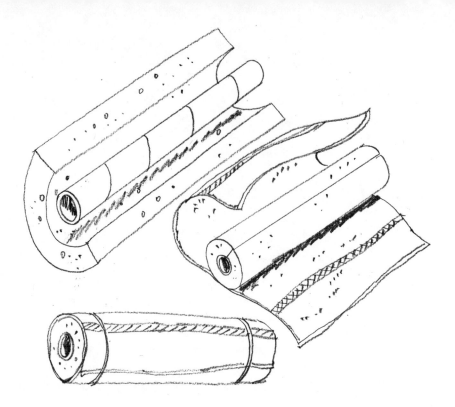

stores, or yard goods stores. Instead of using a piece of foam rubber, you can roll a pillow and hold it together with tape or twine. A towel will make a good cover for the roll. You can keep the towel in place by using rubber bands or snaps.

A *wedge* is very useful for keeping your child in the right position when

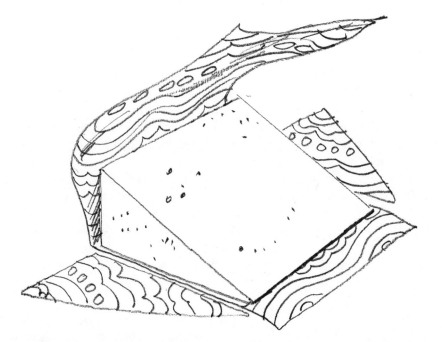

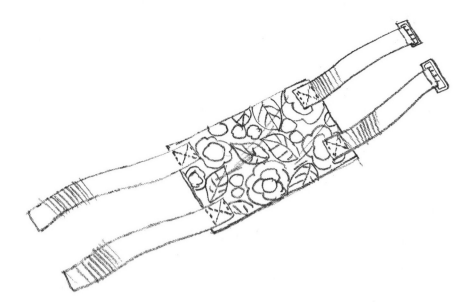

he is on his stomach. A large, wedge-shaped piece of foam rubber can be bought at a discount department store and covered with cloth or vinyl. Or, you can make a wedge out of plywood, cover it with foam rubber, and use the same type of removable vinyl or cloth cover.

If the belt you use across your child's lap does not give him enough support when he sits in a chair, an *extra wide belt* across his chest may help. You can make an extra wide belt by attaching four straps to a piece of cloth to make one wide belt. Make sure the cloth is wide enough—at least six inches. The straps can be tied, buckled, or snapped around your child. You can buy the straps at hospital equipment stores.

CHAIRS

Learning to sit correctly is very important for your child. You should be sure that he sits in a chair that is the right size and will give him enough support. If a chair isn't the right size, there are certain things you can do to make it fit him better.

For example, if the chair seat is so large that your child's knees don't bend at the edge of the seat, you can place a firm cushion or padded board behind him. This will move him forward and allow his knees to bend over the seat of the chair as they should. If the seat is too wide, a cushion or a sandbag can be used to make it narrower. If the child's feet do not reach the floor, place a box or blocks of some kind under his feet to give them support. If his head falls back, cushions or pillows should be placed behind it for support.

Besides regular chairs, there are other things you can use as chairs. Things like rubber inner tubes, heavy cardboard boxes, "corner chairs," and beanbag chairs make good chairs. They let your child sit in positions different from when he is in a regular chair. Changing his position by letting him sit in different kinds of chairs will keep him from getting stiff. Also, he might enjoy sitting on the floor where he can be with other children.

A *rubber inner tube* can be used as a chair for your child. He can sit comfortably in the center of the inner tube if you use pillows or sandbags to prop him up. If you don't have an old inner tube around the house, you can buy one at an auto supply store.

A *heavy cardboard box* can also be used as a chair for your child. The box should be small enough to hold him up in a sitting position. A pillow should be used to support his neck and back. Cut down the front and sides of the box so that he can see what is happening around him. Use masking tape over the cut edges to make them strong and smooth.

You may be able to build a *corner chair* at home out of plywood. Round off one corner on three pieces of plywood. Nail or screw the three pieces together to make the corner seat. Make sure that the base of the seat is large

enough so that your child cannot tip it over. Add a strap to give him support if necessary.

For the older child there is the *MED Corner Sitter,* available in hospital equipment stores. This will help you position your child properly when you go somewhere. It provides both support and freedom and will allow your child to sit at a level where he can play with friends or pets. It is lightweight and waterproof, and folds flat so that it can fit into most cars or be carried by hand.

Beanbag chairs are hard to make, but you can buy them at most department or furniture stores. They are useful because they can be pushed into the shapes your child needs to support his body.

GIVING YOUR CHILD MOBILITY

Moving a handicapped child around takes time and work. It isn't always fun, particularly as he gets older, and as you get older—and maybe a little less strong, too.

Today all sorts of improved devices are at your disposal, however, for "transporting" your child. We will name just a few. Many of these items are

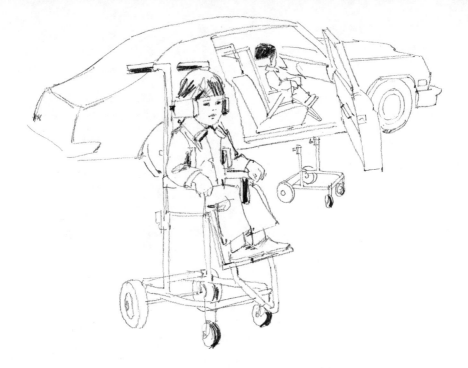

advertised in a magazine called *The Exceptional Parent.* Before trying a new technique or buying a piece of equipment, talk to your child's doctor or therapist to see how his handicap affects the way he is moved. Your child's therapists and teachers will also often have the latest and best information available.

An example is the Bobby Mac baby chair, which is advertised as being three chairs in one. It can be used as a high-chair for an infant, an untippable baby seat, and even a chair in which your baby can nap. Bobby Mac also makes some special carseats and strollers that seem to be sturdy and easily adaptable to multiply handicapped children.

Invacare Exceptional Children's Products makes all sorts of chairs, prone boards, crawlers, canes, posture aids, even shower chairs. Some of these will make it easier for you to take your child places.

If you are not sure of what you want for your child, a place called Abbey Rents (phone 800 421 1170) will send you a catalog from which you can order by phone or mail. They can help you find a chair, stroller, or other support either on a sales or rental basis. If you want to try things out before buying, this may be a way to do it. There are many other suppliers of medical equipment who will also rent things or let you try them before buying. Some of them deal exclusively in equipment for the physically handicapped.

WHEELCHAIRS

Wheelchairs make it easier to move your child. And they give his body support, which is important. Wheelchairs can be bought through hospital equipment stores, but before buying one, think about these points. The wheelchair should

1. help your child do as much for himself as possible
2. be sturdy enough for inside or outside activities
3. be lightweight and easy to fold up
4. have brakes and seatbelts
5. have removable parts which can be easily cleaned or replaced when broken
6. have a vinyl seat for easy cleaning
7. be easily repaired nearby
8. be adjustable
9. be comfortable

Always try out a wheelchair before you buy it. Seat your child in it to see if it's the right size. Pull his hips back so that he is resting on his bottom when he sits, and then look to see if his knees bend over the edge of the seat. Check to make sure that his feet are flat on the footrests and his arms are resting comfortably on the armrests. If all of these points check out, the chair is probably the right size for your child. If at all possible, also have your child's therapist or teacher look at the chair.

There are attachments you can add to a wheelchair to give your child's body more support. For example, an adjustable headrest might help your child hold his head up. Also, if you put a tray on your child's chair, it will give him a place to rest his arms and play with his toys.

The doctor or therapist may decide that a regular wheelchair will not work for your child. He may need one that tilts back or is more adjustable than a regular wheelchair. Relaxation chairs, although not really wheelchairs, do have small wheels and can be rolled around the house. They can be used in an upright position or tipped back. You can also adjust the depth of the chair seat and the height of the footrest.

If your child is able to manage somewhat by himself and you want to help him have fun, there is the Amigo Mini Unit, a motorized wheelchair that is called a "friendly wheelchair." It's made for all sizes and lets your child drive about a bit.

The Mulholland Child Traveler chair is particularly recommended for those getting in and out of cars a lot. It is portable and allows your child to pivot from the chair's base into the car with his seat in a way that can help him feel independent and able to do things for himself.

CAR SEATS

It is important to have a *car seat* that keeps your child safely in his seat while the car is moving. Both General Motors and Ford dealers sell car seats for small children. The GM Loveseat is one of the better seats for multiply handicapped children. It is made of padded plastic and will fit in most cars. The General Motors seat can also be taken out of the car and used as a chair at home. See page 106 for a list of recommended car seats.

WALKING AIDS

Scooters can provide good crawling exercise for children. Ask your child's therapist or teacher if you should try one with your child. You can make a scooter at home fairly easily. Attach four furniture casters to a square or rectangular piece of plywood. (You can buy the casters in a hardware store.) Then glue or tack a block of foam rubber to the top of the plywood so that your child can lie on it comfortably. The scooter should support your child's body from his chest to just below his waist. It should be the right size so that he can use his arms and legs freely to move himself around. If you don't want to build the scooter yourself, you can buy one from a hospital equipment store.

Stand-in tables provide back, head, and arm support for children who are learning to stand. By using the stand-in table, your child learns to put weight on his feet and practices balancing himself. Stand-in tables can be bought in hospital equipment stores.

Walking parallel bars help children who are learning to walk. The child can hold on to the bars as he practices walking between them. You may be able to make parallel bars at home out of iron pipe. There are directions for making the bars in a book by Isabel Robinault, *Functional Aids for the Multiply Handicapped* (New York: Harper & Row, 1973). Also, you can buy parallel bars from a hospital equipment store.

EATING AIDS

A *rubber-coated spoon* will help you feed a child who has a bite reflex or tongue thrust. You can buy one in the baby section of a department store.

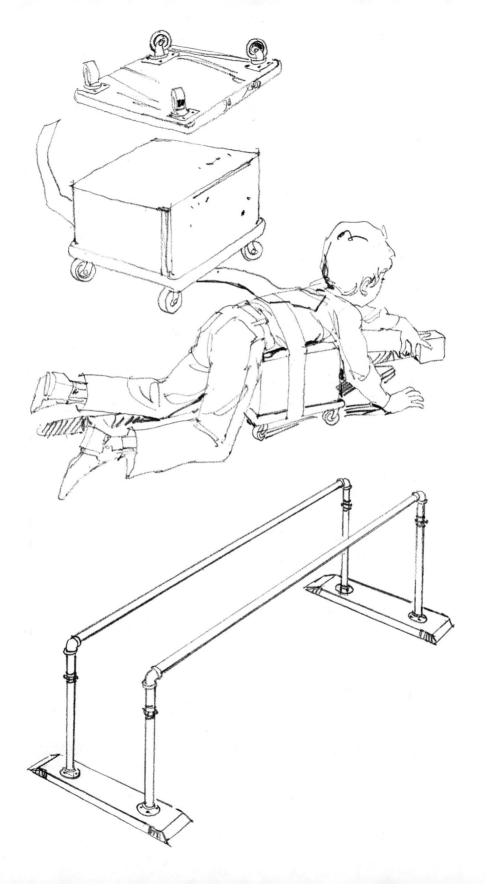

Your child may have trouble holding his spoon in his hand correctly while he is eating. If this happens, you should try to buy a spoon with an extra large handle. You can also make the handle of a regular spoon bigger by pushing the handle through a rubber ball, or by building up the handle by wrapping it with foam rubber and tape.

Your child may push a lot of food off his plate while he is eating. If this happens, you can buy plates with built-up edges to keep the food from falling off. You can also buy a *food guard* that hooks around the edge of the plate and helps keep the food on it. Most of these guards are about one-inch high and are made of stainless steel.

To keep a dish from falling off the table, you can use a *nonslip placemat* or a *suction holder*. The placemats are made out of plastic material with a nonslip surface. The suction holders have a soft rubber base with suction cups on each side that hold the dish to the table.

Special spoons, forks, plates, food guards, placemats, and suction holders can all be bought in hospital equipment stores.

There are many special *nipples* and *drinking aids* that can help your child. For example, the Nuk-Sauger Nipple helps children who have difficulty sucking and swallowing. Two aids for bottle feeding are the Sit-N-Sip Straw or the Sit-Up Straw. These straws are pushed into the bottle and let the child sit up to suck. Some of these drinking aids can be bought in food stores or drugstores. For others, you will have to go to a hospital equipment store.

TOILET TRAINING AIDS

Many different kinds of *potty-chairs* are on the market. The plastic and metal ones are easier to clean than the chairs made of wood. Plastic potty-chairs can be bought at local department or toy stores. Special potty-chairs for physically handicapped children have armrests, footrests, headrests, and

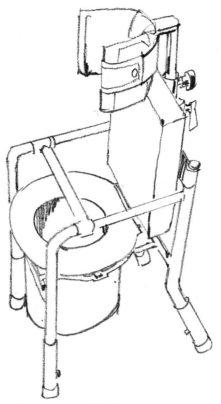

seatbelts which can help your child sit the way he should. You can buy these at hospital equipment stores.

CLOTHING

If your child falls often, you will want to use a *safety helmet* to protect his head. You can buy these helmets at hospital equipment stores. They come in several sizes, so make sure you buy one that fits correctly.

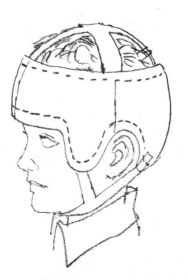

Incontinent pants are padded, waterproof underpants that will help protect your child's clothing if he is not toilet trained. You can buy them at hospital equipment stores and drugstores.

Buttons or zippers may be hard for your multiply handicapped child to use. If this is the case, a self-adhering cloth called *Velcro tape* can be used. Simply sew a piece of tape on each side of the clothing. Then, the clothing can be opened or closed by pulling the pieces apart or pushing them together. There are several different types of Velcro tapes; some pull apart more easily than others. This allows you to make the fastening as easy or as difficult to open as you want.

HYGIENE AIDS

If your child has trouble holding a *toothbrush,* try to make the handle bigger by wrapping foam rubber and tape around it as you did with the spoon handle. An elastic or Velcro strap can also help the child who has difficulty holding on to the handle.

A *Toothette* can be used as a substitute for a toothbrush for children who have tender gums. Instead of stiff bristles, it has a soft sponge tip. The Toothette can be thrown away after use. Don Hare Supply Company (Box 176, Skippack Pike, Skippack, Pa. 19474) sells the Toothettes.

A *flexible shower hose* can help you reach those hard-to-wash places on your child. It can be particularly helpful if your child has to lie in the bathtub or sit in a special bathtub seat. You can buy these at local hardware or department stores.

A *tub seat* can help to support a child who has difficulty sitting up in the bathtub. You can buy tub seats at hospital equipment stores. Or you may be able to make a tub seat out of a plastic laundry basket. There are directions for making the seat in the book by Isabel Robinault mentioned earlier, *Functional Aids for the Multiply Handicapped.*

A specially designed *tub lift* requires minimum effort for the person doing the lifting and gives maximum comfort to your child. It has a seat made of waterproof fabric and a motor or mechanical device to lower the seat into the tub. You can buy these at hospital equipment stores.

HOSPITAL EQUIPMENT STORES

If an item cannot be bought from a local hospital equipment store (look in the yellow pages), you may want to order it through the mail. One company that sells many of these things is J. A. Preston, 71 Fifth Avenue, New York, N.Y. 10003. (Telephone: 212 225 8484.) There is a $3.00 service charge for orders under $50.00.

Transportation

In most states parents of severely or multiply handicapped children can get a special automobile license plate. With this plate, you can park in spaces marked "Handicapped Parking Only." You may also be allowed to park in some "no parking" areas for up to 90 minutes, but you'd better check with the local police. There is no extra charge for this special license plate. Write to your state's motor vehicle bureau for information.

Moving your child from the car to the house may be difficult if you can't find a nearby parking space. If it is hard to find a parking space on the street near your home, speak to your local police. It may be possible to have signs put up in front of your house that will keep other cars from parking there.

Try to seat your child in the safest place in the car. In case of a crash or sudden stop, a child is safer in the back than in the front seat. However, if you are the only adult in the car, it may be necessary to place your child in the front seat in case he needs your help in the event of a seizure or other emergency.

Holding a child in your lap while you are riding as a passenger is not safe. In the event of a crash or even a sudden stop, the chances are great that he will be thrown from your arms.

If your child has developed adequate sitting balance, adult seat belts are the best available protection. Do not use a shoulder belt until the child is tall enough that the belt does not cross his head or neck.

Car seats should meet Federal Safety Standard Number 213. This can be determined by checking the label. The following seats were recommended after being tested by the Consumer's Union and the Highway Safety Research Institute, 1973.

Bobby-Mac by Colliers—Reclinable infant carrier-child seat.
> Child size: for the child from birth to 35 pounds and up to 40 inches tall
> Available at: department stores

Peterson #74—Molded plastic bucket seat; converts with different modules to fit child—infant faces rearward, toddler faces front with shield; child over 35 pounds uses harness.

Child size: for child from birth to 4 years

Available at: department stores

Infant Carrier—Deep container of 1-piece molded plastic. Faces backward.

Child size: for infants from birth to 20 pounds (approximately 1 year old)

Available at: Chevrolet, Pontiac, Oldsmobile, Buick, Cadillac, Plymouth-Dodge-Chrysler dealers; some department stores

G.M. Loveseat—Conventional seat; raises child up slightly, restrains with 5-point harness, one buckle.

Child size: for child that has outgrown infant loveseat; designed for a child 1–4 years; 20–40 pounds

Available at: Chevrolet, Pontiac, Oldsmobile, Buick, and Cadillac dealers and some department stores

Ford Tot-Guard—Seat cushion and padded plastic shield.
    Child size: for the child from approximately 25–50 pounds
    Available at: Ford Motor Company dealerships

Kantwet Care Seat (#784 and 884)—Traditional-looking seat, considerably upgraded, 5-point harness, anchor strap installed or fastened with rear lap belt if used in front seat.
    Child size: for child who can sit alone, up to 45 pounds
    Available at: department stores

Infantseat Auto Restraint Harness—5-point harness with one buckle; anchor strap must be permanently installed or attached with rear lap belt when used in front seat.
    Child size: for child who can sit alone; to 52 pounds
    Available at: department stores

Your county's Mental Health/Mental Retardation Unit (listed under county services in the phone book) can be a valuable information resource. They can tell you about a variety of services, including public and private transportation for your child and special bus or taxi services for the handicapped. Other local agencies for the handicapped can also inform you about this.

The Mental Health/Mental Retardation Unit may help you pay the costs of transportation for your child. For example, if you need a cab to take your child to the doctor, the unit may pay the cost. How much they contribute depends on how much you are able to pay.

A new law, effective September 30, 1978, requires cities to purchase "transbuses" if they get federal transportation funds from Washington. Transbuses are vehicles with a low (17-inch) floor, wide doorways, and ramps for wheelchairs. They will be a great help to all the handicapped. If you live in or near a city and have any questions about public transportation services for the handicapped, a good place to call is your local regional office of the Urban Mass Transportation Administration (listed under United States Government, Department of Transportation, in your phone book).

It is also important for you to know how your local ambulance service, police station, and fire company can help. For example, you should know if they will come to your house if you have to call in an emergency. Some ambulance services will come only if they are requested by a doctor, and will only take patients to a specific hospital—not necessarily the one you request.

Babysitting

This section will help you find a babysitter who is used to working with handicapped children. When the babysitter comes to your house, you should have certain information ready for her. We have included here suggestions on what kinds of information you should give her.

FINDING A BABYSITTER

Your local chapter of the National Association for Retarded Citizens (NARC) may run training programs for babysitters to take care of handicapped children. Call your local chapter to find out.

Often, other parents of multiply handicapped children will know good babysitters. You can meet other parents by joining parent groups at your child's school or at your local NARC chapter. Also, you and other parents of multiply handicapped children can take turns babysitting.

There may be teenagers in the neighborhood who would be interested in learning how to care for handicapped children. Perhaps you can get them to attend the NARC training program.

Sometimes the Mental Health/Mental Retardation Unit can help you find a babysitter. If you need to be away from your child for more than a day, call your Mental Health/Mental Retardation Unit and ask for help. Be sure that you ask for respite care and make it clear how long you will need this help. Call several weeks before the time when you will be away.

INFORMATION FOR THE BABYSITTER

When the babysitter comes to your house, have the information she will need ready for her. Fill out a form like the one we have suggested here,

"What the Babysitter Should Know." It will tell your babysitter what special things she needs to know and what she must do in an emergency. It is a good idea to have one copy of the form in your child's bedroom and another near the phone.

WHAT THE BABYSITTER SHOULD KNOW

Emergency Information

Our name _____ Child's name _____

Home address _____ Phone # _____

WHERE WE WILL BE: _____
(name, address, phone #)

If you can't reach us, call _____
(name, address, phone #)

Sickness: Call me.

_____
(special instructions)

IF CHILD IS SICK OR HURT: Call Doctor _____
(name & phone #)

    or Doctor _____
(name & phone #)

If you can't get a doctor, call Ambulance at _____
(phone #)

    or Police at _____
(phone #)

Call Mrs. _____ at _____

Then call me.   (neighbor)   (phone #)

Fire: Get child out of house. Call Fire Department at _____
(phone #)

POLICE: _____
(phone #)

Special Instructions

Medicine: _____
(Drug)   (How much)   (when to give)

_____
(Drug)   (How much)   (when to give)

Meals: _____
(Type of food)   (When)   (Restrictions)

_____
(Feeding methods)

Toileting: _____

Sleep: _____
(Time for bed)   (Special Instructions)

Play: _____
(Where)   (Toys)   (Avoid)

Other Instructions: _____

_____

My Child's Favorite _____
(Activity)   (Food)   (Other)

65

Income Tax Deductions

The Internal Revenue Service allows income tax deductions for some of the expenses of caring for your handicapped child. Make sure you take all of the deductions you should receive. One way to do this is to keep a careful record of all the money you spend in caring for your child. This should include

1. the name and address of the people to whom the payment was made
2. the date of the payment
3. the amount of money paid
4. the reason for the payment

When it comes time to file your tax return, use these records to figure out your deductions. A letter from your child's doctor telling about her condition should be attached to your return. Mail a copy of this with your tax return and keep a copy with your cancelled checks and bills.

You can deduct the costs of

1. Medical and dental treatment. This includes what you pay the doctor and dentist and the cost of things like eye examinations, hearing tests, X-rays, medicine, vitamins, special foods prescribed by the doctor, etc.
2. Special schools or sheltered workshops, if the main purpose is to help handicapped children. This can include the cost of tuition and room and board.
3. Special evaluations and training. This includes the cost of psychological tests and special instructions or training such as speech instruction.
4. Transportation of your child to and from special schools and institutions, hospitals, and doctors' offices. This can include the cost of taxis, buses, and trains. Or, if you drive her in your own car, you may also deduct a certain amount per mile plus the parking and toll fees. Call the Internal Revenue Service to find out how much you can deduct.

5. Medical insurance. Call the Internal Revenue Service to find out how much of the cost of medical insurance you can deduct.

6. Special equipment, if the doctor says that your child needs it because of her handicap. This includes eyeglasses, hearing aids, crutches, braces, wheelchairs, air-conditioning for children with asthma, and other types of equipment for the home or automobile. You can deduct the cost of installing special equipment such as the air-conditioning. Disposable diapers and diaper service are also deductible.

7. Child care. If you are divorced, widowed, or married to a disabled person, and if you are employed, you may deduct part of the cost of help you hire to care for your child. Check with the Internal Revenue Service for the latest information.

For more information about tax deductions, write or call for the following booklets:

"Checklist of Medical Expense Deductions"
United Cerebral Palsy Association, Inc.
66 East 34th Street
New York, New York 10016

"Deductions for Medical and Dental Expenses"
and "Child Care and Disabled Dependent Care"
Your local Internal Revenue Service office

"Facts You Should Know About Tax Deductions for Your Handicapped Child"
Coordinating Council for Handicapped Children
407 South Dearborn Street
Chicago, Illinois 60605

Planning for the Future

Planning for the future is especially important for parents who have a severely handicapped child. Who will be able to care for your child if you are not able to? How will you be able to support your child when you retire?

This section has some of the answers to these questions. You will find the information helpful, but you should also seek legal or other professional help.

Much of the following information can be found in "How to Provide for Their Future," a booklet available from the National Association for Retarded Citizens (NARC) P.O. Box 6109, 2709 Avenue E East, Arlington, Texas 76011.

DEATH OF PARENTS

In most states, there are laws that see that a child under the age of 21 will be taken care of when his parents die. But at age 21, the child is expected to be able to take care of himself. Most severely handicapped persons cannot take care of themselves when they become adults. Therefore, the parents of a handicapped child should talk to a lawyer to make sure their child will be taken care of when they die or are disabled. This should be done as soon as possible.

WILLS AND TRUSTS

The severely handicapped person cannot handle large amounts of money or property. So the parent should not will money or property directly to the child, and should ask relatives not to do so either.

A will can be used by a parent to make financial plans for the child and to make sure that he is cared for in the future. One way to do this is to set up a

114

trust in which a third party (a relative, lawyer, or bank, for example) oversees the disposal of your child's property. Make plans now for a trust by talking to a lawyer or bank officer.

INSURANCE

Life insurance on the parents' lives is one way of taking care of the child if the parents die.

Group policies are available. The National Association for Retarded Citizens (NARC), for example, offers term insurance at group rates for the parents of retarded children. This plan is available to a parent if he is earning an income, is under 70, and is a member of a local or state unit of NARC.

In addition to life insurance, a parent would be wise to have family health and accident insurance. When the child is too old to be covered under the family policy (usually at age 19), it may be necessary to obtain an individual policy. In some states, a child who is still dependent upon the parents after age 19 can remain on the family policy.

SOCIAL SECURITY

When a parent dies or retires, a severely handicapped child can receive social security payments. Any child can get these payments until he reaches 18 years of age. But a handicapped child may still receive them after he reaches 18. He can get these monthly payments as long as his condition keeps him from "substantial gainful work" as an adult. The size of the payments depends upon how much the father or mother has paid into the social security fund. You can get information on these benefits from the social security office.

Other programs may provide aid to your handicapped child or your family. Ask about Supplementary Security Income (SSI) at your nearest social security office, and about medical aid programs at your county Board of Assistance office.

There are also aid programs designed for children of veterans who are at least 50 percent disabled as a result of service in the Armed Forces, or who have died. A veteran's multiply handicapped child is eligible for these benefits. Call your nearest Veteran's Administration office (listed under Veteran's Administration in the telephone book).

LEGAL HELP

It is important to have legal help when writing a will or setting up a trust fund. If a parent does not have a family lawyer and needs help to find one, he can get a list of lawyers from the local bar association's Lawyer Reference Service.

All states and most communities have legal assistance programs for people who cannot afford private legal help. If you cannot afford to pay for a lawyer, contact the local Legal Aid Society or the local bar association.

PART IV

Equal Education and
the Severely Handicapped

In this section of the book we will be talking about some legal matters that have a very significant part to play in your child's education. It is now federal law that public schools provide your handicapped child with a free and appropriate public education. We think it's important that you understand some of the history behind the law, as well as what the law provides to serve you and your child.

Here we have sketched out the kinds of rights you and your child have under the present law. And we have discussed the procedures which are now used in schools for identifying, evaluating, and serving handicapped children. The Individualized Education Program (or IEP) is explained, too. Though some of these things are complicated, we don't expect you to become lawyers to understand them. But, by being informed about these legal matters, you can help your child achieve the education to which she is now entitled by law.

Introduction: Lawsuits and Litigation

For many years, severely handicapped children were not allowed to take part in the educational programs of public schools. It was felt that these children would not be able to benefit from the programs provided. Most people also believed that the more severely handicapped children could not be educated, and thus school laws allowed the school districts to exclude children they felt could not benefit from attending school.

Now, things have changed drastically. A flood of lawsuits has begun to make clear the government's responsibility to the handicapped children in this country. The suits have dealt with the rights of handicapped children to

a free public school education which would meet their special needs. The individuals who filed these suits did so because their previous efforts as a group failed to get educational programs for handicapped children.

In 1971, one such lawsuit was brought by the parents of 13 mentally retarded children against the state of Pennsylvania. The parents were represented by the Pennsylvania Association for Retarded Children. This case, *Pennsylvania Association for Retarded Children* v. *Commonwealth of Pennsylvania,* was the first of a series of important lawsuits. It ended in a Consent Agreement ordered by the court between the Pennsylvania Association for Retarded Children and the Commonwealth of Pennsylvania. The following were the major points of the agreement:

1. No mentally retarded child is to be denied access to a free public program of education and training while he is less than 21 years of age.
2. The parents have the right to notification and an opportunity for a hearing when any educational program is suggested or before any change in educational assignment takes place. (This is referred to as *due process procedure.*)

Many experts were called to testify in the Pennsylvania case. And what they said made it clear that retarded children could benefit from programs of education and training that were designed to meet their special needs. In fact, if they were given such an education, most would be able to be self-sufficient, and the remaining few would benefit by gaining self-care skills. Clearly, the experts felt that denying handicapped children this opportunity was a violation of a basic right, that of *equal protection under the law.* By giving the right of due process to these children, the court was responding to the Fourteenth Amendment, which states that "no state may deprive any person of life, liberty, or property without due process of law." This right protects a person from arbitrary and unreasonable action. The Pennsylvania case set the tone for the other lawsuits and legislation that quickly followed.

The next important suit was aimed at the District of Columbia and concerned the rights of all handicapped children: *Mills* v. *Board of Education of District of Columbia.* This suit was filed to force the school district to provide an appropriate education for retarded, physically handicapped, emotionally disturbed, and all other handicapped children. It stated that the school district was not providing enough funds to meet the needs of handicapped children. In addition, the suit stated that these children were not being included in educational programs, that they were often suspended and assigned to different programs, and that the parents were not properly notified or given the opportunity to object to changes and suggest other ones. That is, parents were not being granted their basic right of due process of law.

During the summer of 1972, the federal court declared that exceptional children have a right to a public education, and ordered the District of Columbia to offer all exceptional children an appropriate education within 30 days.

These two lawsuits set the stage for what was to happen during the next five years. Many states followed Pennsylvania and the District of Columbia and passed legislation that granted these rights. Other states were sued and entered into agreements similar to Pennsylvania's. The outcome of these actions on behalf of handicapped children was President Ford's signing in November 1975 of Public Law 94-142, The Education for All Handicapped Children's Act.

This is one of the most significant laws ever to affect the education of handicapped children. It is important to parents of severely handicapped children because for years their children were excluded from programs provided by public schools. The Act is even more important because it clearly indicates the role parents must play in deciding what kind of education the child will have.

Free, Appropriate
Public School Education

The schools in this nation must now, by law, provide a free, appropriate public school education to all handicapped children, even the most severely handicapped. Moreover, the parents of a handicapped child must now take an active part in developing the educational program and must also approve the program before it can be put into practice.

It might be helpful at this point to give you an example of the process for determining the placement and educational program for a handicapped child. This will help you to understand your rights and responsibilities as a parent.

IDENTIFICATION

Parents of severely physically handicapped children know that their child is handicapped long before the child is of school age. However, there are conditions such as hearing impairment or delayed language development which the parents may not be aware of immediately. And in some cases the parent may know that the child is handicapped but may be unaware of how her handicap will affect her learning until the child enters school. For these reasons the school becomes involved in the process of identifying handicapped children.

Typically, a parent becomes aware of a school's programs through discussions with other parents, advocacy groups, or advertisements on radio, on television, or in newspapers. These sources direct the parent to a local "child find," sponsored by the state's Department of Education. The people working on the "child find" project will be able to give you information

about specific services provided by local school districts, including a person to contact about securing these services for your child. Some states provide services for handicapped children from birth to 21 years of age. Other states begin at age three, and still others begin when services are provided to "normal" children. For example, if a school district provides programs for four-year-olds, then the district must also provide a program for a handicapped child of the same age. In any case, if you call the Department of Education in your state, they will provide all the information necessary to enroll your handicapped child in an appropriate public school program.

EVALUATION

When a child is thought to be handicapped, she must be evaluated so that you, her teacher, and her therapist may fully understand the nature of her problem to plan ways of helping her. But before any evaluation can take place, the school must inform you that your child will be evaluated. This evaluation will probably include an individual intelligence test, individual behavioral studies to determine the child's social and emotional status, medical testing to determine her physical capabilities, and tests by any other qualified person that would be helpful in determining your child's individual needs.

NOTICE OF INTENT TO CONDUCT AN EVALUATION

ORIGINATOR: Special Education Administrator.

PURPOSE: To inform parents that a referral for an evaluation has been made and to inform parents of their rights.

Date: _____

Dear Parent:

_____ _____
(Name)   (Title)
recently filed a form requesting that your child, _____
                                                          (Child's name)
evaluated by this office for potential special education and related services. A copy of the request as filed is enclosed for your review.

The evaluation procedures and their associated instruments that will be used in each of the following areas are:

Assessment Areas	Evaluation Procedures	Associated Instruments
Intelligence:		
Achievement:		
Behavior:		
Physical:		
Other:		

The findings of the evaluation will be used by the following people to develop a set of program recommendations for your child.

Name	Title
Name	Title
Name	Title

It is very important that you be aware of and understand that you have the following rights:
1. To review all records related to the referral for evaluation.
2. To review the procedures and instruments to be used in the evaluation.
3. To refuse to permit the evaluation (in which case the local education agency can request a hearing to try to overrule you).
4. To be fully informed of the results of the evaluation.
5 To get an outside evaluation for your child from a public agency, at public expense if necessary.

You child's educational status will not be changed without your knowledge and written approval.

Enclosed is a Parent Permission Form which must be completed by you and returned to this office within 5 school days.

Should you have any questions please do not hesitate to call me at _____

Yours truly,

Enclosures: Form 1
            Form 5   _____
                              Name
                              Title

124

Name of Administrator of Special Education:_____ (This information could _____

Address: _____ be printed in advance.) _____

_____

Phone Number:_____

Dear (Director of Special Education):

I am in receipt of the Notice of Intent to Conduct an Evaluation for my child, _____(child's name)_____.
I understand the reasons and the description of the evaluation process that you provided and have checked the appropriate box below.

☐ Permission is given to conduct the evaluation as described.

☐ Permission is denied.

_____
Parent's Signature

_____
Date

   To develop an appropriate program for your child, information from all sources must be considered. The federal law states, "No one test or type of test is (can be) used as the sole criterion for placement." Also, the tests and other evaluation material that are given must be in your child's native language or other appropriate mode of communication. Each local education agency must make sure that the evaluation is fair to the child.

   Before any evaluation can begin, you, as a parent, must give your permission. You can give permission only after the school fully explains the evaluation activity in your native language or other appropriate means of communication. You must agree in writing before the evaluation can be given. Before you sign, you should receive a description of the types of tests and procedures that will be used, and why they were chosen.

   When the evaluation is completed, the school will notify you of the results in writing. We suggest that you discuss these results in a conference at the school. This will make it easier for you to understand what the results mean to your child's educational program.

   If you do not agree with the evaluation results, or if you feel you should have an additional evaluation, you have the right to obtain an *independent educational evaluation*—at your own expense. (This evaluation may be at public expense, if the school agrees.)

   The independent evaluation is given by a certified or licensed examiner who is employed neither by your state nor the school district responsible for your child's education. If you have the additional evaluation, the results

125

Originator: Any professional conducting assessments for the purpose of determining a child's eligibility for special education and related services.

Purpose: To summarize assessment information and present performance levels for the development of the child's individualized education program.

p._____ of _____

Assessment
Performed by: _____
　　　　　　　　　　　　Name　　　　　　　　　　　　Position _____

　　　　　　　　　_____
　　　　　　　　　　　　Address　　　　　　　　　　Specialized Field _____

　　　　　　　　　_____
　　　　　　　　　　　　Phone　　　　　　　　　　　_____

Student's Name: _____　　　Birth Date _____

Date of Report: _____

Specific questions to be addressed:

Assessment Tools and Settings
(Check the tests administered)

WISC	Spache	Slosson	Winterhaven	WAIS
Date__ /__ /__	Date__ /__ /__	Date__ /__ /__	Date__ /__ /__	Date __/ __/__

Leiter	WIPPSI	WISC R	Bender-Gestalt
Date__ /__ /__	Date__ /__ /__	Date__ /__ /__	Date__ /__ /__

Other Diagnostic Tools

1.
2.
3. etc.

*Results	*Implications for IEP	* Present Level(s) of Performance Statements

*Additional information should be attached to this page if required.

Signature_____　　Date _____
　　　　　　　Specialist

must be considered by the state and local educational agency in planning the placement and program for your child.

THE INDIVIDUALIZED EDUCATION PROGRAM (IEP)

Special education can involve a wide variety of programs and services. These may take place in a variety of settings—in public or private schools or in special education centers—and may be called resource rooms, itinerate programs, or self-contained special classes. It is important for you to under-

stand both the specific program that is to be given to your child and something about the environment (location) in which the program will take place. The program, placement, and environment go together in what is called the *Individualized Education Program,* or IEP.

The federal law makes it clear that the state and local education agency must guarantee that "an individualized education program is provided for each handicapped child who is receiving or will receive special education." This means that each handicapped child will have a program developed to meet her individual needs.

Each local education agency must develop or revise an IEP for every handicapped child at the beginning of the school year, and the school must review and revise the IEP at least once a year.

The local education agency must hold a meeting to develop and discuss the IEP which is being written for your child. The meeting must include the following people:

1. a representative of the local education agency who is qualified to provide or supervise special education services for your child (This is generally a supervisor or coordinator of special education.)

127

2. your child's teacher or teachers (regular or special or both) who will have direct responsibility for carrying out the IEP
3. you, as the parent of the child
4. any other individual whom you, the parent, feel can be helpful

If it is appropriate, your child can also attend. It is important for you to participate in this and any other meetings related to the IEP. The meetings must be held at a time and place agreed upon by all participants. Often they are scheduled in the evening to allow both parents to attend.

The final IEP should be written at such a meeting so that everyone involved in the child's education has the chance to make suggestions. The purpose is to develop a specific program containing annual goals for your child, short-term instructional objectives, means and schedules for evaluation of the program, and resources required for the program. The program must be directly related to your child's strengths and weaknesses that were determined during her evaluation.

As we mentioned before, each local education agency must see that the parents are given the chance to participate in each meeting. You should make every effort to attend these meetings, since you know your child better than anyone else. You can certainly add much information and direction in developing an IEP.

In addition, the local education agency must be certain that you, as a parent, fully understand the proceedings at the meeting. An interpreter may be present for parents who are deaf or whose native language is not English.

If you cannot attend, the local education agency will involve you through an individual or conference telephone call, if possible. The agency may develop the IEP without you if you are unwilling or unable to participate. In cases like this, the local education agency will keep a record of its attempts to encourage your participation. They may even ask you to sign a statement to allow them to go ahead and develop the IEP.

CONTENT OF AN IEP

Each state and local education agency develops IEP forms and formats to meet its needs. However, the law requires that certain elements be contained in all IEPs. All IEPs must include

1. *A statement of your child's present level of educational performance.* This includes her academic achievement, social adaptation, prevocational and vocational skills, psychomotor skills, and self-help skills. This statement is based on school records and the evaluation that precedes the development of the IEP.

INDIVIDUALIZED EDUCATION PROGRAM

School District
Responsible _____

Date(s) of meeting: _____

_____

_____

Current
placement _____

Eligibility
certified _____
                (date)

Period of individualized education program

_____ to _____

Persons present	Relationship to child

Curriculum areas* requiring special education and related services	Present Level(s) of performance	Annual goals	Short term objectives	Time required	Objectives attained (dates)		
Area 1							
Area 2							

*If more space is required, use an additional sheet.

A. List any special instructional material or media necessary to implement this individualized education program.

Special education and related services recommended	Personnel responsible (name and title)	Date services begin	Duration
Curriculum area 1			
Curriculum area 2			

(continued on page 130)

2. *A statement of goals to be reached by the end of the school year through your child's educational program.* We must stress here that the purpose of the IEP is not to evaluate a teacher's performance, but rather to provide a plan the teacher and other professionals can use in carrying out the educational program.

129

(continued from page 129)

B. Describe the extent to which the child will participate in regular education programs.

_____

_____

_____

_____

C. Recommended type of placement: _____
   (include physical education)

D. Provide justification for the type of educational placement.

_____

_____

_____

_____

E. Actual placement: _____

_____

F. List the criteria, evaluating procedures and schedule for determining whether the short term objectives are met.

Short term objectives	Objective criteria	Evaluation procedures	Schedule

Date of parental acceptance/rejection _____

Signature _____

Signature _____

3. *A statement of short-term instructional objectives.* These are steps between your child's present level of educational performance and the annual goals. These objectives should be measurable.

4. *A statement of specific educational services needed by your child.* This statement must be based on what your child actually needs and not just upon what is available. This involves a description of all the special education and related services and any special instructional materials

and media needed, the date the services will begin, the length of time the services will be given, a description of how much time your child will spend in regular class programs, who will be involved in providing her program, and an evaluation schedule.

We must stress that the IEP is a joint effort to develop a program to meet the needs of your child. It is based upon all the information gathered during the evaluation. Parents play an important part in this development, and you should make every effort to be a part of the IEP team. Here is what one mother of a handicapped child felt she would like to see included in the IEP:

(1) a statement of my child's present development level in all areas relating to physical, emotional, and intellectual development; (2) a statement of my child's learning strengths; (3) a statement of any medical, environmental, or cultural considerations particular to my child; (4) a statement of my child's education needs and their relationship to the total sequence of developmental skills; (5) a statement of specific goals and timetables; (6) a statement of instructional alternatives; (7) a listing of appropriate educational materials relevant to my child's learning characteristics; (8) a clear delineation of the responsibilities of the entire planning team; (9) established time frames for daily programming, periodic review, and evaluation; and (10) a description of program procedures. [Quoted from the National Advisory Committee on the Handicapped, 1977, p. 8]

In some schools parents will sign the IEP document itself if they agree with the program and placement. Other schools may use a different procedure. Shortly after the meeting, you may receive from the school the IEP and a "due process notice" regarding your child's placement. This notice, which we will explain in detail below, is the means by which the IEP can be implemented.

Once you receive the IEP and placement notice, you have two choices. If you agree with the program, sign the form to show you have been informed of the program/placement and that you agree. Since you and the school have developed the IEP together, you will most likely sign the form when you receive it.

However you may find that you do not agree with the IEP. When this happens, you and the school should make every effort to discuss the points you disagree on and try to solve the problem so that an educational program can be provided for your child as soon as possible. If you cannot agree, you have the right to request a "due process hearing."

REQUEST FOR DUE PROCESS HEARING

Every possible alternative should be tried before a due process hearing is requested. However, if at any time during evaluation, placement, and program, the parents and school cannot agree, a due process hearing is a chance to review and solve the disagreement through a decision by an impartial hearing officer. This officer, representing the chief school officer of the state, is often a special educator or a person with training in a related area and is an expert in the education of handicapped children.

Usually, a due process hearing is held when a change in the child's educational placement is planned and the parent does not agree with the school on these plans. However, a hearing can also be initiated to obtain permission to conduct an evaluation of a child when parents and school disagree.

Within a certain period of time after receiving the request for a hearing (10 to 15 days), the school will schedule the due process hearing, and you will be notified. It will be held in the school district at a time convenient to the parents. If both parents work, the hearing is generally scheduled in the evening hours.

The notice you receive should contain the following information:

1. the time and place of the due process hearing
2. the parents' right to require the attendance of any officer, employee, or agent of the local or state education agency who has relevant information regarding the child
3. the parents' right to be represented at the hearing
4. the right to review school records of their child

The parents may choose to be represented at the hearing by an advocate, education expert, or counsel. Unless the parents request otherwise, it will be a closed hearing.

Each state has its own way of conducting a hearing, but a general procedure is followed. As mentioned earlier, a hearing officer is appointed who is not affiliated with the school. He is responsible for conducting the hearing in a fair manner. The parents and school have the opportunity to present evidence and to ask questions during the hearing, which is recorded verbatim. Both sides have the right to cross-examine, and the hearing officer may also ask questions to get more information or to clarify any points. Accurate information must be provided to allow the hearing officer to determine an appropriate program from the information contained in the records and statements.

The hearing officer will usually open the hearing with a statement identifying himself. Then each person at the hearing will be asked to identify himself or herself for the record and to state the reason for attending the hearing. The representative of the school then gives his opening statement, which is a summary of its position, followed by an opening statement by the parents.

After each side has presented its opening statements, the school presents its case, showing why the program they have proposed is appropriate for the child. After each person presents testimony, the parents, or their representative, may ask questions of those who presented testimony. In addition, the hearing officer may ask questions of any witness. The school also has the right to ask questions of the parents or any witness who represents them. When both sides have finished their presentations, each may give a summary statement, followed by a closing statement by the hearing officer.

During all of these proceedings and until the hearing officer makes a decision, the child must remain in her original (current) educational assignment.

The hearing officer then states the amount of time it will take to reach a decision which will be based upon the evidence and testimony found in the hearing transcript. He also informs the parents and school representatives of the appeal process, in case either party does not agree with his decision.

Once the decision has been reached and mailed to the school and the parents, each has a period of time to appeal. If no appeal is made, the school district is responsible for implementing the program. There is no win-

ate education for the child.

SURROGATE PARENT

In some cases, a child may not have a parent, or the child may be a ward of the state, or a parent may not be available to represent the child in matters concerning her education. In this kind of case, the law states that the child has a right to be represented and, therefore, the state must appoint a "surrogate parent" to represent the child in matters concerning her education.

The definition of surrogate parent may differ slightly from state to state; however, in general, (a) the surrogate must have no interest that conflicts with the interests of the child he represents; (b) the surrogate must have the knowledge and skills to insure adequate representation of the child; and (c) the surrogate parent must not be an employee of the state or local educational agency which is involved in the education or care of the child.

Generally the surrogate parent represents the child in all matters concerning the identification, evaluation, and educational placement of the child. For specific information, contact the Department of Education of your state.

Conclusion

Once your child is placed in a special education program, the process of evaluating his formal education should not end. The IEP, on which the placement was made, should be reviewed periodically, at least once a year. At the time the IEP is reviewed, either the parent or school may decide that the program should be changed and the procedure for approving the placement repeated.

Since the "right to education" movement began in 1972, many legal decisions have affected the education and training of handicapped children. While it is important to be kept informed of the effects of the law on special education, it is more important for you to be aware of the needs of your child and what may be an appropriate program for him.

The procedures outlined in this section will no doubt change with the times; most laws do. So it would be helpful to keep in touch with the happenings in special education by joining an organization that works with parents of handicapped children.

INFORMATION SERVICES

The following agencies can give you additional information on the education of handicapped children and youth, as well as on their legal rights.

The Government Relations Unit
Council for Exceptional Children
1920 Association Drive
Reston, Va. 22091

Human Policy Press
Center on Human Policy
Division of Special Education and Rehabilitation
Syracuse University
Syracuse, N.Y. 13210

The National Center for Law and the Handicapped, Inc.
1235 North Eddy Street
South Bend, Ind. 46617

National Legal Aid and Defender Association
2100 M Street, NW
Washington, D.C. 20037

REVIEW OF INDIVIDUALIZED EDUCATION PROGRAMS

ORIGINATOR: Special Education Administrator.

PURPOSE: No later than 8 months after a child's written educational program has been initiated and during each calendar year thereafter, the local education agency must conduct a review of the individualized education program to evaluate its effectiveness in meeting the child's educational needs. This form letter is to notify the parents when the review is scheduled.

Dear Parent:

It has been almost 8 months (1 year) since_____(Child's name)_____was placed in his current educational program. In order to evaluate how well suited the program is, we have scheduled a review (reevaluation).

The review will take place on _____ at _____
                                                Day   Date   Time

at _____
                                                                          Place

It is important that you participate in this review. If the scheduled time is not convenient please contact me immediately so that we might rearrange it.

The following procedures will occur at the review:

Within 10 days after the reevaluation you will receive notice of the findings and recommendations made.

It is very important that you be aware of and understand that you have the following rights:

1. To go over all records related to the reevaluation.
2. To go over the procedures of the reevaluation.
3. To participate in developing any necessary changes required in the individualized education program.

Should you have any questions please feel free to call me at any time at _____.

Yours truly,

_____
Special Education Administrator

READING LIST

If you would like to learn more about equal education and the severely handicapped, you might consult the following:

Abeson, A. R.; Bolick, N.; and Hass, J. *A Primer on Due Process—Education Decisions for Handicapped Children.* Reston, Va.: Council for Exceptional Children, 1975.

Council for Exceptional Children. *Procedural Safeguards, P.L. 94–142—A Guide for Schools and Parents* (multimedia package). Reston, Va.: Council for Exceptional Children, 1977.

Hobbs, N., ed. *Issues in the Classification of Children.* 2 vols. San Francisco: Jossey-Bass, 1975.

MacFeely, R. W. "The Nuts and Bolts of Procedural Due Process." *Phi Delta Kappan* 57 (1975): 26–27.

National Advisory Committee on the Handicapped. *The Individualized Education Program: Key to an Appropriate Education for the Handicapped Child* (1977 annual report). Washington, D.C.: U.S. Government Printing Office, 1977.

Torres, S. *A Primer on Individualized Education Programs for Handicapped Children.* Reston, Va.: Council for Exceptional Children, 1977.

Torres, S. *Special Education Administrative Policies Manual.* Reston, Va.: Council for Exceptional Children, 1977.

Weintraub, F. J.; Abeson, A. R.; Ballard, J.; and LaVor, M. L. *Public Policy and the Education of Exceptional Children.* Reston, Va.: Council for Exceptional Children, 1976.

PART V

Select Bibliography of
Further Readings

Most of the books, articles, and pamphlets we have cited here are different from those listed in the Reading Lists elsewhere in the book. Some of them are more technical and detailed studies of the subjects we have referred to; others explore problems that may be special to your particular child; still others talk about common problems in simple language and may offer a fresh point of view. All of them, we hope, can be useful to parents who are looking for more specialized information than we could hope to provide within the scope of this book.

Abeson, A.; Bolick, N.; and Hass, J. *A Primer on Due Process: Education Decisions for Handicapped Children.* Reston, Va.: Council for Exceptional Children, 1975. Discusses legal problems, equal education, due process, school law, and student rights.

American Foundation for the Blind. *Directory of Agencies Serving the Visually Handicapped in the United States.* New York: American Foundation for the Blind, 1974. Lists names and addresses of agencies serving the visually handicapped.

American Society of Dentistry for Children. "One Hundred and Twenty-three Most Asked Questions by Parents about Their Children's Teeth." (Reprinted from *Healthcare* 63, 1971). Answers questions about children's teeth, diet, and general dental health. A chapter is dedicated to the dental problems of the handicapped.

Attwell, A. A., and Clabby, D. A. *The Retarded Child: Answers to Questions Parents Ask.* Los Angeles: Western Psychological Services, 1971. Contains information about mental retardation, diagnosis and referral, family problems and adjustments, home training, schooling, parent organizations, institutionalization, and legal provisions.

Baird, H. W. *The Child with Convulsions.* New York: Grune & Stratton, 1972. A text on the diagnosis and treatment of epilepsy.

Barrows, H. S., and Goldensohn, E. S. *Handbook for Parents.* New York: Ayerst Laboratories. Introductory material on epilepsy. (Available from Ayerst Laboratories, 685 Third Avenue, New York 10017.)

Becker, W. C. *Parents Are Teachers: A Child Management Program.* Champaign, Ill.: Research Press, 1971. Shows parents how to systematically teach their children in positive ways.

Bensberg, G. J., ed. *Teaching the Mentally Retarded: A Handbook for Ward Personnel.* Atlanta: Southern Regional Education Board, 1966. Provides information on teaching self-help skills to retarded children.

Bricker, D. "Imitative Sign Training as a Facilitator of Word-Object Association with Low-Functioning Children." *American Journal of Mental Deficiency* 76 (March 1972): 509–516.

Brown, D. L. *Developmental Handicaps in Babies and Young Children: A Guide for Parents.* Springfield, Ill.: Charles C Thomas, 1972. A guide which introduces parents to aspects of developmental handicaps in babies and young children, discusses evaluation, counseling, and agencies which offer assistance.

Cerebral Palsy Clinic. *Patterns for Helmet, Diaper, Wrist and Thigh Cuff, and Restraining Vest.* (Available from Cerebral Palsy Clinic, Indiana University Medical Center, Indianapolis, Indiana 46202)

Cohen, S., and Levitt, E. *Nighttime and Your Handicapped Child: Prevention and Handling of Sleep Problems.* New York: Special Education Development Center, City University of New York, Hunter College. (Available from NARC, 2709 Avenue E East, P.O. Box 6109, Arlington, Tex. 76011)

Dean, D. "Closer Look: A Parent Information Service." *Exceptional Children* 41 (May 1975): 527–530. Explains origin, services, and goals of this organization.

Dental Guidance Council for Cerebral Palsy. *Dentistry for the Handicapped.* New York: Dental Guidance Council for Cerebral Palsy. Includes seven articles and three pamphlets. Among these are "Your Handicapped Child Needs Dental Care Now," "Bulletin of the Dental Guidance Council for Cerebral Palsy," and "Is Premedication Necessary for Handicapped Children?" (Available from Dental Guidance Council for Cerebral Palsy, 122 East 23rd Street, New York, N.Y. 10010)

Exceptional Parent. "Income Tax Guide." *Exceptional Parent* 4 (November/December 1974): 28–30. A guide to acquaint parents with procedures of claiming deductions for children with disabilities.

Feldman, M.; Byalick, R.; and Rosedale, M. "Parents and Professionals: A Partnership in Special Education." *Exceptional Children* 41 (May 1975): 551–554. Explains parent involvement in a nontraditional educational setting for multiply handicapped.

Finnie, N. *Handling the Young Cerebral Palsied Child at Home.* New York: E. P. Dutton, 1975. A complete guide to home care of the cerebral palsied child.

Foxx, R. M., and Azrin, N. H. *Toilet Training the Retarded: A Rapid Program for Day and Nighttime Independent Toileting.* Champaign, Ill.: Research Press, 1974. Gives detailed information on how to toilet train your child. Makes suggestions about use of various kinds of toilet training devices such as potty-chairs and pants alarms.

Fryberger, Y. B. *Sitter's Course for Handicapped Individuals.* Cincinnati, Ohio: Cincinnati Center for Developmental Disorders, 1974. Material and information used in a sitter's course for handicapped individuals. Useful for parents wishing to teach a friend how to sit for their handicapped child.

Green, A. A. "Preventive Guide for Multi-Handicapped Children: Dental Care Begins at Home." *Rehabilitation Literature* 31 (1970): 10–12.

Hannam, C. *Parents and Mentally Handicapped Children.* London: Penguin Books, 1975. An informal description of the effect on family life of having a retarded child.

Hart, V. *Beginning with the Handicapped.* Springfield, Ill.: Charles C Thomas, 1974. Gives parents information about self-care skills, motor development, adaptive behavior, and communication.

Haslam, R., ed. *Pediatric Clinics of North America: Habilitation of the Handicapped Child.* Philadelphia: W. B. Saunders Co., 1973. A listing of pediatric clinics in North America.

Herron, R. G. "Volunteer Parent Groups in Special Education." *Thrust for Educational Leadership* 2 (May 1973): 11—15. Explores role and activities of parent groups by using the California Association for the Retarded as an example.

Joyce, M., ed. *Rights of the Physically Handicapped: A Layman's Guide.* Marshall, Minn.: Southwest State University, 1976. A catalog, listed by state, of laws which affect the physically handicapped, and a summary of federal programs.

Keen, R. A., and Sullivan, S. "Motor Programming for the Severely Handicapped." In *Assessment and Curriculum for the Severely Handicapped,* edited by E. Somerton and K. Turner. Reston, Va.: Council for Exceptional Children, in press.

Kent, L. *Language Acquisition Program for the Severely Retarded.* Champaign, Ill.: Research Press, 1974. A detailed guide to systematic language instruction.

Klein, S. D. "How to Evaluate Residential Schools." *Exceptional Parent* 3 (May–June 1973): 43–46. Practical guidelines for parents in selecting a school for their child.

Kroth, R. "Facilitating Educational Progress by Improving Parent Conferences." *Focus on Exceptional Children* 4 (December 1972): 1–10. Ways to establish parent-teacher cooperation through conferences.

Lopez, L. V., ed. *Education Directory.* Washington, D.C.: U.S. Government Printing Office. An annual directory which lists the names and addresses of educational associations and their chief officers.

Macey, P. G. *Mobilizing Multiply Handicapped Children: A Manual for the Design and Construction of Modified Wheelchairs.* Lawrence, Kansas: Division of Continuing Education, University of Kansas, 1974. A construction manual for modifying wheelchairs to fit a child's individual needs.

Massachusetts Council of Organizations of the Handicapped. *A Directory of Organizations of the Handicapped in the United States.* Hyde Park, Mass.: Massachusetts Council of Organizations of the Handicapped, 1974. A geographically arranged listing of self-help organizations for the physically and mentally handicapped throughout the country.

McCraven, C. J. *An Advocacy Manual for Parents of Handicapped Children.* Washington, D.C.: U.S. Government Printing Office, 1976. Describes laws pertaining to the handicapped in California, social security benefits, and methods to assure that the state is providing the services it should.

Menolascino, F. J., and Pearson, P. H., eds. *Beyond the Limits: Innovations in Services for the Severely and Profoundly Retarded.* Seattle, Wash.: Bernie Straub Publishing & Special Child Publications, 1974. Describes the existing and emerging trends in helping severely handicapped children. Discusses the personal conflicts of parents and the role of parent associations in obtaining services for the mentally retarded.

Molloy, J. S., and Matkin, A. M. *Your Developmentally Retarded Child Can Communicate.* New York: John Day, 1975. Contains material for teaching communication skills to nonverbal children.

National Association for Retarded Citizens. *Facts on Mental Retardation.* Arlington, Texas: National Association for Retarded Citizens, 1973.

Describes mental retardation and how the National Association for Retarded Citizens is working to meet the needs of retarded individuals.

National Easter Seal Society for Crippled Children and Adults. *The Easter Seal Directory of Resident Camps for Persons with Special Health Needs.* 4th ed. Chicago: National Easter Seal Society for Crippled Children and Adults, 1975. A list of 250 resident camps by state, with an alphabetical index by name. Camps are identified as to physical, mental, social, and emotional disabilities served.

Personnel Training Program for the Education of the Severely Handicapped. "Parent Training." In *Educational Technology for the Severely Handicapped.* Topeka, Kansas: Neurological Institute, 1975. A bibliography for parents of the severely handicapped.

President's Committee on Mental Retardation. *In Service to the Mentally Retarded.* Washington, D.C.: President's Committee on Mental Retardation, 1970. A listing of voluntary agencies and their interest in the mentally retarded.

Robinault, I., ed. *Functional Aids for the Multiply Handicapped.* New York: Harper & Row, 1973. A resource book about equipment for the handicapped: how to select it, how to use it, and where to buy it.

Shoob, D. *A Community Respite Care Program for the Mentally Retarded or Physically Handicapped.* Springfield, Va.: Childcare Assistance Program, 1975. A book to motivate parents and others to develop respite care programs in their community.

Somerton, E., and Turner K., eds. *Assessment and Curriculum for the Severely Handicapped.* Reston, Va.: Council for Exceptional Children, in press.

United Cerebral Palsy Association, Inc. *Tomorrow Is Today: Planning Ahead for Long-term Care, Legally and Financially.* New York: United Cerebral Palsy Association, Inc. Assists parents in planning for the future of their handicapped child by giving advice on financial planning and legal assistance.

Vanderheiden, G., and Luster, M. *Illustrated Digest of Nonvocal Communication and Writing Aids for Severely Physically Handicapped Individuals.* Trace Center, University of Wisconsin-Madison, 1977. A comprehensive presentation of communication aids and how to use them.

Wabash Center for the Mentally Retarded, Inc. *Guide to Early Developmental Training.* Lafayette, Ind.: Wabash Center Sheltered Workshop, 1973. A curriculum guide which includes motor development, cognitive development, language development, self-care, and glossary of terms.

Watson, L. S., and Bassinger, J. F. "Parent Training Technology: A Potential Service Delivery System." *Mental Retardation* 12 (October 1974):

3–10. Describes an approach which utilizes parents as behavior modification technicians to teach self-help, language, motor coordination, and social and academic skills to handicapped children.

Weiner, F. *Help for the Handicapped Child.* New York: McGraw Hill, 1973. Describes in detail public and private services for each handicapping condition, including treatment and prognosis. Each chapter has a glossary of terms frequently used in connection with the handicap described.

Wentworth, E. H. *Listen to Your Heart: A Message to Parents of Handicapped Children.* Boston: Houghton Mifflin, 1974. A look at the special problems parents need to cope with in raising handicapped children.

Wicks, D., and Falk, M. L. *Advice to Parents of a Cleft Palate Child.* Springfield, Ill.: Charles C Thomas, 1970. Comprehensive study which offers information and understanding to parents concerning the future of a child with a cleft palate and/or cleft lip.

Index